Weight Watchers®

Slim Ways™

HEARTY MEALS

Macmillan • USA

Weight Watchers

Since 1963, Weight Watchers has grown from a handful of people to millions of enrollments annually. Today, Weight Watchers is the recognized leading name in safe, sensible weight control. Weight Watchers members form a diverse group, from youths to senior citizens, attending meetings virtually around the globe.

Weight-loss and weight-management results vary by individual, but we recommend that you attend Weight Watchers meetings, follow the Weight Watchers food plan and participate in regular physical activity. For the Weight Watchers meeting nearest you, call 1-800-651-6000.

Thanks to everyone who helped put this cookbook together: recipe developers Luli Gray, Kathleen Hackett and Tamara Holt; recipe editor Patricia Barnett; nutrition consultants Lynne S. Hill, M.S., R.D., L.D., and William A. Hill, M.S., R.D., L.D.

Editor-in-Chief: Lee Haiken
Book Editor: Martha Schueneman
Cover photo by Martin Jacobs
Cover photo: Hungarian Goulash Soup

MACMILLAN
A Simon & Schuster Macmillan Company
1633 Broadway
New York, NY 10019-6785

MACMILLAN is a registered trademark of Macmillan, Inc.
WEIGHT WATCHERS and SLIM WAYS are registered trademarks of Weight Watchers International, Inc.

Library of Congress Cataloging-in-Publication Data
Weight watchers slim ways hearty meals.
        p.   cm.
    Includes index.
    ISBN 0-02-861295-7 (alk. paper)
    1. Reducing diets--Recipes.   2. Entrées (Cookery)   I. Weight
Watchers International.
RM222.2.W3276   1996
641.5'635--dc20   96–11095
                                                                          CIP

Manufactured in the United States of America
10 9 8 7 6 5 4 3 2 1

CONTENTS

INTRODUCTION

Remember those winter afternoons when you'd come home from ice-skating? Your cheeks would be red, your fingers and toes practically numb, but the smells wafting from the kitchen seemed to warm you up before you had your boots off. Whether it was thick beef and vegetable stew, piping hot chicken pot pie or rich, cheesy lasagna, it was delicious, stick-to-your-ribs fare—a real hearty meal, lovingly prepared from a family recipe passed down through the generations. You've probably thought you'd never be able to eat like that again while staying within the nutritional guidelines you know you should . . . until now!

"Hearty" is a word that isn't often used to describe foods that are reduced in fat, in sodium and in cholesterol, but it's probably the type of meal most health-conscious people would admit they miss the most. In *Weight Watchers Slim Ways Hearty Meals*, we've taken 150 favorite recipes and given them "nutritional makeovers." Our lightened versions cut down on fat and calories without compromising flavor. Readily available fresh herbs and vegetables; "aromatics" like onion, garlic and fresh ginger root; leaner meats; less oil for sauteing and, where appropriate, low- or nonfat dairy products all help to turn long-forbidden favorites into trusted recipes you'll enjoy over and over again.

You'll find Old-World favorites like Cassoulet and Sauerbraten Stew, and New-World dishes like Tamale Pie and Jambalaya; there is also "All-World" fare like African Beef and Plantain Stew, Teriyaki Beef with Mushrooms and Caramelized Onions, Moroccan Lamb Tagine and Paella. Here are recipes for traditional American dishes, too, like New England Boiled Dinner, Yankee Pot Roast, Meatloaf with Peppers and Gravy, Oyster Po' Boy with Rémoulade Sauce and Brunswick Stew.

We even give you new twists on old classics—try Asian Stuffed Peppers or Pot Roast with Mustard and Sun-Dried Tomatoes if you're looking for something beyond the ordinary—as well as meatless and vegetarian dishes: Spinach and Cheese Cannelloni, Red Pepper, Onion and Tomato Frittata and Butternut Squash Chili are among our favorites.

In *Weight Watchers Slim Ways Hearty Meals*, you'll find simple recipes for familiar foods that reflect our contemporary healthful lifestyles.

1

BEEF

STANDING RIB ROAST

Makes 8 servings

Prime rib, a luxurious cut of beef generally high in both flavor and cost, makes a superb treat. The tomato-wine sauce in this wonderfully seasoned version makes it even more special, and the leftovers become terrific sandwiches. For a less expensive version, substitute a 1-pound 14-ounce boneless lean beef eye round roast.

4 large garlic cloves, minced
1 teaspoon dried thyme leaves
$^1/_2$ teaspoon freshly ground black
    pepper, or to taste
$^1/_4$ teaspoon ground red pepper, or
    to taste
One 3-pound 8-ounce bone-in beef
    rib roast, tied with kitchen
    string*

2 medium onions, minced
$^1/_2$ cup stewed tomatoes, pureed
$^1/_2$ cup low-sodium beef broth
4 fluid ounces ($^1/_2$ cup) dry red wine
1 teaspoon Worcestershire sauce

1. To prepare roast, in small bowl, combine garlic, thyme and black and ground red peppers; set aside. Place roast onto work surface, bone-side down; with thin-bladed sharp knife, pierce roast 12 times, making 1" deep evenly spaced cuts on top side of roast. With fingertips, spread each cut open and stuff with $^1/_2$ teaspoon garlic mixture; seal cuts by smoothing with fingertips. Spread any remaining seasoning mixture over roast. Place roast into gallon-size sealable plastic bag; seal bag, squeezing out air. Refrigerate roast overnight.
2. Remove roast from refrigerator; let stand 30 minutes.
3. Preheat oven to 375° F. Spray rack in roasting pan with nonstick cooking spray.
4. Place roast onto prepared rack, bone-side down; roast 1–1$^1/_4$ hours, until cooked through and meat thermometer inserted into center of roast not touching bone registers 140° F for rare, 155° F for medium. Transfer roast to cutting board; cover to keep warm.

A 3-pound 8-ounce bone-in rib roast will yield about 1 pound 8 ounces boneless cooked beef.

5. Meanwhile, to prepare sauce, spray large nonstick skillet with nonstick cooking spray; heat. Add onions; cook over medium heat, stirring frequently, 8–10 minutes, until onions are golden brown. Stir in tomatoes, broth and wine; bring liquid to a boil. Cook, stirring constantly, 5 minutes, until mixture is reduced in volume to about 1 cup; stir in Worcestershire sauce.

6. Carve beef into 8 equal portions; arrange on serving platter. Serve with sauce.

Serving (3 ounces beef with 2 tablespoons sauce) provides: $^1/_2$ Vegetable, 3 Proteins, 15 Optional Calories.

Per serving: 224 Calories, 11 g Total Fat, 4 g Saturated Fat, 68 mg Cholesterol, 115 mg Sodium, 4 g Total Carbohydrate, 1 g Dietary Fiber, 24 g Protein, 27 mg Calcium.

BOILED BEEF WITH HORSERADISH SAUCE

Makes 8 servings

This classic entrée takes a little time, but you get a delicious hot meal, great leftovers for sandwiches as well as broth that is satisfying either on its own or as the base for a hearty soup.

2 pounds chicken necks, backs and wings
1 pound 14 ounces boneless lean beef rump roast
2 cups low-sodium chicken broth
2 cups low-sodium beef broth
$1/2$ teaspoon salt
4 medium celery stalks, coarsely chopped
2 medium onions, coarsely chopped
1 medium carrot, coarsely chopped
6 fresh flat-leaf parsley sprigs

1 bay leaf
8 whole black peppercorns
2 whole allspice
$1/2$ teaspoon vegetable oil
$1/4$ medium onion, minced
1 tablespoon all-purpose flour
$1/4$ cup apple cider or juice
2 tablespoons prepared drained horseradish, squeezed dry
$1 1/2$ teaspoons cider vinegar
Freshly ground black pepper, to taste
2 tablespoons nonfat sour cream

1. To prepare beef and broth, in large pot or Dutch oven, combine chicken, beef, chicken and beef broths and salt; add enough cold water to cover chicken and beef. Bring liquid to a boil; with slotted spoon, skim off foam that accumulates on surface. Reduce heat to low; cook, continuing to skim off accumulated foam, 30 minutes (do not boil).
2. Meanwhile, in large nonstick skillet, combine celery, coarsely chopped onions and carrot; cook over medium heat, stirring frequently, 8–10 minutes, until onions are golden brown.
3. Transfer vegetable mixture to beef mixture; stir in parsley, bay leaf, peppercorns and allspice. Cook, partially covered, 3 hours, until beef feels tender when pierced with fork. Transfer beef to cutting board; cover to keep warm.
4. Place medium sieve over medium bowl. Strain broth through sieve, reserving liquid; discard solids. Let broth stand 15–20 minutes, until fat accumulates on top; with paper towels or large spoon, remove fat.

5. To prepare sauce, in medium nonstick saucepan, heat oil; add minced onion. Cook over medium heat, stirring frequently, 3–5 minutes, until onion is softened. Reduce heat to low; sprinkle onion mixture with flour. Cook, stirring constantly, 2 minutes, until flour is dissolved. With wire whisk, stir in cider, horseradish, vinegar, pepper and ³/₄ cup of the reserved broth; continuing to stir, cook 10 minutes, until mixture is thickened and flavors are blended. Remove from heat; blend in sour cream.
6. To serve, in small saucepan, cook ¹/₂ cup of the remaining reserved broth* over high heat 2 minutes, until slightly reduced in volume. Thinly slice beef across the grain. Arrange beef on serving platter; top with reduced broth. Serve with horseradish sauce.

Serving (3 ounces beef with 1 scant tablespoon reduced broth and 2¹/₂ tablespoons sauce) provides: 3 Proteins, 25 Optional Calories.

Per serving: 166 Calories, 6 g Total Fat, 2 g Saturated Fat, 62 mg Cholesterol, 149 mg Sodium, 3 g Total Carbohydrate, 0 g Dietary Fiber, 24 g Protein, 17 mg Calcium.

One cup broth provides: 20 Optional Calories.

Per serving: 20 Calories, 1 g Total Fat, 0 g Saturated Fat, 0 mg Cholesterol, 303 mg Sodium, 1 g Total Carbohydrate, 0 g Dietary Fiber, 4 g Protein, 10 mg Calcium.

* Divide remaining broth into 1-cup portions; cool, then freeze, covered, until solid. Use in recipes calling for beef or chicken broth, or serve on its own.

YANKEE POT ROAST

Makes 12 servings

This robust dish will satisfy the heartiest appetites; serve it with mashed potatoes flavored with the plentiful gravy.

$^1/_2$ teaspoon freshly ground black pepper

$^1/_4$ teaspoon ground allspice

$^1/_4$ teaspoon ground anise seed

$^1/_4$ teaspoon ground coriander

One 2-pound 13-ounce boneless lean top or bottom round beef roast

4 medium onions, coarsely chopped

1 medium celery stalk, coarsely chopped

$^1/_2$ medium carrot, coarsely chopped

2 large garlic cloves, peeled

1 teaspoon vegetable oil

3 cups low-sodium beef broth

$^1/_2$ cup low-sodium tomato juice

1. Preheat oven to 450° F. Spray medium roasting pan with nonstick cooking spray.
2. In small bowl, combine pepper, allspice, anise seed and coriander; rub into beef on all sides. Refrigerate, covered, 15 minutes.
3. In prepared roasting pan, combine onions, celery, carrot and garlic; spray lightly with nonstick cooking spray. Roast vegetable mixture, stirring once, 10–15 minutes, until onions are golden brown. Remove vegetable mixture from oven; set aside. Reduce oven temperature to 250° F.
4. In large nonstick skillet, heat oil; add seasoned beef. Cook over medium heat, turning as needed, until browned on all sides. Transfer browned beef to roasting pan with vegetable mixture; set aside.
5. To same skillet, add 2 cups of the broth; cook, scraping up browned bits from bottom of skillet, 5 minutes, until heated through and well combined. Pour broth mixture, remaining 1 cup broth and juice over beef; bake, covered, basting every 30 minutes with pan juices, 3 hours, until beef feels tender when pierced with fork or meat thermometer inserted into center of beef registers 175° F. Transfer beef to cutting board; cover to keep warm.
6. To prepare gravy, place medium sieve over medium saucepan; strain vegetable mixture through sieve. Let liquid stand 15–20 minutes, until fat accumulates on top; with paper towels or large spoon, remove fat. Transfer solids to blender or food processor; purée, adding 1 tablespoon liquid at a time, if necessary, until smooth, reserving any remaining liquid in saucepan.

7. Place same sieve over same saucepan; strain vegetable purée through sieve. Discard any solids remaining in sieve; bring gravy to a boil. Reduce heat to low; simmer, stirring occasionally, 5 minutes, until flavors are blended.
8. Meanwhile, thinly slice beef across the grain. Arrange beef on serving platter; top with $1^1/2$ cups gravy. Serve with remaining gravy on the side.

Serving (3 ounces beef with $^1/_4$ cup gravy) provides: $^1/_2$ Vegetable, 3 Proteins, 10 Optional Calories.

Per serving: 201 Calories, 5 g Total Fat, 2 g Saturated Fat, 77 mg Cholesterol, 97 mg Sodium, 4 g Total Carbohydrate, 1 g Dietary Fiber, 32 g Protein, 14 mg Calcium.

POT ROAST WITH MUSTARD AND SUN-DRIED TOMATOES

Makes 4 servings

Make this roast on a cold winter weekend; the long, slow cooking allows the flavors to develop and tenderizes the meat.

1 teaspoon olive oil
15 ounces boneless lean beef
   eye round steak
2 fluid ounces (¹/4 cup)
   brandy
2 cups low-sodium beef broth
6 medium shallots, sliced

2 sun-dried tomato halves (not
   packed in oil), thinly sliced
3 tablespoons coarse-grain mustard
1 tablespoon Dijon-style mustard
3 garlic cloves, thinly sliced
Pinch freshly ground black pepper,
   or to taste

1. Preheat oven to 325° F.
2. In large heatproof pot or Dutch oven, heat oil; add steak. Cook over medium heat, turning once, until browned on both sides. Remove steak from pot; set aside.
3. In same pot, cook brandy 5–7 minutes, until syrupy. Add broth, shallots, tomato, coarse-grain and Dijon-style mustards, garlic and pepper; stir to combine. Bring liquid to a boil; remove from heat.
4. Add steak to broth mixture, turning to coat; bake, covered, basting steak occasionally with broth mixture, 1¹/2–2 hours, until steak is cooked through and very tender.
5. Transfer steak to cutting board; let stand 10 minutes. Thinly slice steak; arrange steak slices on serving platter. Serve with broth mixture.

Serving (3 ounces steak with one-fourth of broth mixture) provides:
¹/4 Fat, ¹/2 Vegetable, 3 Proteins, 50 Optional Calories.

Per serving: 233 Calories, 6 g Total Fat, 2 g Saturated Fat,
57 mg Cholesterol, 298 mg Sodium, 6 g Total Carbohydrate,
0 g Dietary Fiber, 27 g Protein, 16 mg Calcium.

Swiss Steak with Gravy

Makes 4 servings

Swiss steak makes a homey meal, especially served with mashed potatoes or wide noodles and some chocolate pudding for dessert. Both novice and expert cooks alike will love this easy-to-prepare version.

1 tablespoon + 1 teaspoon all-purpose flour	1 cup tomato sauce (no salt added)
1 teaspoon paprika	2 medium onions, minced
$^1/_2$ teaspoon freshly ground black pepper	$^1/_2$ medium celery stalk, minced
Pinch garlic powder	$^1/_4$ medium carrot, minced
One 15-ounce piece boneless lean beef round steak ($^3/_4$" thick)	$^1/_4$ medium green bell pepper, minced
	1 slice crisp-cooked bacon, crumbled
1 cup low-sodium beef broth	$^1/_4$ teaspoon dried marjoram

1. Preheat oven to 300° F.
2. On sheet of wax paper or paper plate, combine flour, paprika, $^1/_4$ teaspoon of the black pepper and the garlic powder. Add steak, turning to coat evenly; rub flour mixture into steak. Cut steak into 4 equal pieces.
3. In medium heatproof skillet, cook steak over medium heat, turning once, 8–10 minutes, until browned on both sides and cooked through. Add broth, tomato sauce, onions, celery, carrot, bell pepper, bacon, marjoram and remaining $^1/_4$ teaspoon black pepper; cook, scraping up browned bits from bottom of skillet, 5 minutes, until heated through and well combined. Bake, covered, $1^1/_2$–2 hours, until beef is very tender. Divide evenly among 4 plates and serve.

Serving (3 ounces steak with $^1/_2$ cup gravy) provides: $1^3/_4$ Vegetables, 3 Proteins, 25 Optional Calories.

Per serving: 214 Calories, 6 g Total Fat, 2 g Saturated Fat, 63 mg Cholesterol, 123 mg Sodium, 12 g Total Carbohydrate, 2 g Dietary Fiber, 27 g Protein, 20 mg Calcium.

MATAMBRE

Makes 10 servings

Matambre means "kills hunger" in Spanish, and this luscious Argentine stuffed roast will do just that. Serve it hot, with rice pilaf and a garlicky salad of greens, scallions, cooked artichoke hearts and green beans. Or try this dish cold, sliced $1/4$" thick, with mustard and nonfat mayonnaise stirred into the sauce.

One 2-pound 3-ounce boneless lean beef round steak (1" thick), sliced horizontally to form a pocket
1 teaspoon freshly ground black pepper
1 teaspoon olive oil
1 medium onion, thinly sliced
$1/2$ medium carrot, minced
$1/4$ cup low-sodium beef broth
Two 10-ounce packages thawed frozen chopped spinach, thoroughly drained and squeezed dry

2 eggs, hard-cooked and sliced
2 teaspoons unseasoned meat tenderizer
$1/2$ cup packed fresh flat-leaf parsley leaves
$1/2$ cup red wine vinegar
$1/4$ cup packed fresh cilantro leaves
1 medium jalapeño pepper, seeded, deveined and minced (wear gloves to prevent irritation)

1. Preheat oven to 350° F. Spray medium roasting pan with nonstick cooking spray.
2. Sprinkle steak pocket evenly with $1/2$ teaspoon of the black pepper; set aside.
3. In large nonstick skillet, heat oil; add onion and carrot. Cook over medium heat, stirring frequently, 6–7 minutes, until onion is lightly browned. Add broth; bring liquid to a boil. Reduce heat to low; simmer 3 minutes, until liquid is evaporated. Remove from heat; stir in spinach.
4. Stuff beef pocket with half of the spinach mixture; top filling evenly with egg slices. Spread remaining spinach mixture over eggs. Tie steak with kitchen string at 1" intervals.
5. Moisten both sides of steak with water; sprinkle evenly with meat tenderizer. With tines of fork, pierce steak all over, about $1/2$" apart. Place steak into prepared roasting pan; roast, basting occasionally with pan juices, $1^{1}/_{2}$–2 hours, until steak is cooked through and very tender. Transfer steak to cutting board; cover to keep warm.

6. Meanwhile, to prepare sauce, in blender or food processor, combine parsley, vinegar, cilantro, jalapeño pepper, $^1/_4$ cup water and remaining $^1/_2$ teaspoon black pepper; purée until as smooth as possible. Let stand 30 minutes.

7. Cut steak into 10 equal portions; arrange on serving platter. Serve with sauce.

Serving (1 slice stuffed steak with 2 tablespoons sauce) provides:
1 Vegetable, 3 Proteins, 5 Optional Calories.

Per serving: 182 Calories, 7 g Total Fat, 2 g Saturated Fat,
100 mg Cholesterol, 484 mg Sodium, 5 g Total Carbohydrate,
2 g Dietary Fiber, 25 g Protein, 157 mg Calcium.

BRASCIOLE IN TOMATO SAUCE

Makes 4 servings

Here is an old-fashioned southern Italian dish; serve it on a bed of rigatoni or penne with a sprinkle of cheese. For its intense flavor, be sure to use real Parmigiano-Reggiano cheese in this dish.

One 15-ounce piece boneless lean beef round steak ($^{1}/_{2}$" thick)
1 teaspoon olive oil
$^{1}/_{2}$ medium onion, minced
$^{1}/_{4}$ medium celery stalk, minced
2 garlic cloves, minced
$^{1}/_{3}$ cup + 2 teaspoons plain dried bread crumbs
3 tablespoons minced fresh flat-leaf parsley

3 tablespoons grated Parmigiano-Reggiano cheese
$^{1}/_{2}$ teaspoon dried oregano
$^{1}/_{4}$ teaspoon freshly ground black pepper
$^{1}/_{4}$ teaspoon salt
1 cup tomato sauce (no salt added)
1 cup stewed tomatoes, pureed
$^{1}/_{2}$ cup low-sodium beef broth

1. To prepare brasciole, place steak between 2 sheets of wax paper; with meat mallet or bottom of heavy saucepan, pound steak to $^{1}/_{8}$" thickness. Remove and discard wax paper; set steak aside.
2. Preheat oven to 300° F. Spray 8" square baking pan with nonstick cooking spray.
3. In medium nonstick skillet, heat oil; add onion, celery and garlic. Cook over medium heat, stirring frequently, 3–5 minutes, until onion is softened.
4. Transfer onion mixture to small bowl; add bread crumbs, 2 tablespoons of the parsley, 2 tablespoons of the cheese, the oregano, pepper and salt. Spoon crumb mixture onto one end of steak to within $^{1}/_{2}$" of edge; carefully roll steak, jelly-roll fashion, to enclose filling. Tie steak roll at 1" intervals with kitchen string. Place roll into prepared baking pan; bake 15 minutes.
5. Meanwhile, to prepare sauce, in small bowl, combine tomato sauce, stewed tomatoes and broth; pour over steak roll. Bake, basting every 15 minutes with sauce, $1^{1}/_{2}$–2 hours, until beef is cooked through and very tender.
6. With spatula, carefully transfer brasciole to serving platter; top with sauce, remaining 1 tablespoon parsley and remaining 1 tablespoon cheese. Cut brasciole into 4 equal portions; serve with sauce.

Serving (one-fourth of brasciole with one-fourth of sauce) provides:
$^1/_4$ Fat, $1^3/_4$ Vegetables, 3 Proteins, $^1/_2$ Bread, 25 Optional Calories.

Per serving: 260 Calories, 8 g Total Fat, 3 g Saturated Fat,
65 mg Cholesterol, 493 mg Sodium, 18 g Total Carbohydrate,
3 g Dietary Fiber, 28 g Protein, 102 mg Calcium.

NEW CHEESE STEAK

Makes 4 servings

This version of the ever-popular Philadelphia cheese steak sandwich has all the flavor of the original but a lot less fat. Fresh vegetables and herbs make this sandwich filling enough to satisfy a hearty appetite but light enough to enjoy often.

2 tablespoons balsamic vinegar
1 garlic clove, minced
One 8-ounce boneless lean beef loin or round steak ($3/4$" thick)
2 teaspoons olive oil
$1^1/2$ medium onions, sliced
$1^1/2$ medium tomatoes, diced
$1/2$ teaspoon salt
$1/2$ teaspoon freshly ground black pepper
One 8-ounce loaf French bread
3 ounces provolone or part-skim mozzarella cheese, thinly sliced
$1/4$ cup minced fresh basil

1. To prepare marinade, in quart-size sealable plastic bag, combine vinegar and garlic; add steak. Seal bag, squeezing out air; turn to coat steak. Refrigerate 20 minutes, turning bag occasionally.
2. Drain and discard marinade.
3. Spray large nonstick skillet with nonstick cooking spray; heat. Add steak; cook over medium heat, turning as needed, 15–18 minutes, until browned on all sides and just cooked through. Transfer steak to cutting board; cover to keep warm.
4. In same skillet, heat oil; add onions. Cook over medium heat, stirring frequently, 8–10 minutes, until onions are golden brown. Add tomatoes; cook, stirring frequently, 2–3 minutes, until warm. Sprinkle vegetable mixture with salt and pepper; stir to combine. Remove from heat; set aside.
5. Preheat broiler.
6. Split bread lengthwise almost all the way through; spread open. Slice steak very thinly; place steak slices evenly along bottom half of bread; top evenly with cheese. Place bread, filled-side up, onto broiler pan; broil 4" from heat, 3–4 minutes, until cheese is melted.
7. Spoon vegetable mixture evenly over cheese; sprinkle evenly with basil. Gently close bread; cut crosswise into 4 equal portions and serve.

Serving (one-fourth of loaf) provides: $1/2$ Fat, $1^1/4$ Vegetables, $2^1/2$ Proteins, 2 Breads.

Per serving with provolone cheese: 361 Calories, 13 g Total Fat, 5 g Saturated Fat, 48 mg Cholesterol, 845 mg Sodium, 36 g Total Carbohydrate, 3 g Dietary Fiber, 24 g Protein, 243 mg Calcium.

Per serving with mozzarella cheese: 340 Calories, 11 g Total Fat, 4 g Saturated Fat, 46 mg Cholesterol, 758 mg Sodium, 37 g Total Carbohydrate, 3 g Dietary Fiber, 23 g Protein, 219 mg Calcium.

SLICED STEAK SALAD

Makes 4 servings

This salad is filling, yet light enough to enjoy in the heat of the summer. It makes a wonderful lunch or dinner for family or guests.

2 tablespoons red wine vinegar
1 tablespoon olive oil
2 teaspoons minced fresh rosemary leaves
$^1/_2$ teaspoon freshly ground black pepper
$^1/_2$ teaspoon salt
2 medium tomatoes, diced
4 cups torn arugula or spinach leaves
1 pound cooked all-purpose potatoes, cut into wedges
8 ounces cooked lean flank steak, thinly sliced
2 cups sliced mushrooms

1. To prepare dressing, in small jar with tight-fitting lid or small bowl, combine vinegar, oil, rosemary, pepper and salt; cover and shake well or, with wire whisk, blend until combined.
2. Place tomatoes into large bowl. Pour dressing over tomatoes; toss to combine. Let stand 20 minutes.
3. Add arugula, potatoes, steak and mushrooms to tomato mixture; toss gently to combine. Divide evenly among 4 plates and serve.

Serving (2 cups) provides: $^3/_4$ Fat, 4 Vegetables, 2 Proteins, 1 Bread.

Per serving: 254 Calories, 8 g Total Fat, 2 g Saturated Fat, 28 mg Cholesterol, 373 mg Sodium, 30 g Total Carbohydrate, 5 g Dietary Fiber, 16 g Protein, 78 mg Calcium.

ROAST BEEF AND BEET SALAD WITH ORANGES

Makes 4 servings

The flavors in this salad hail from Mexico. Although the combination sounds unusual, it is delectable.

4 cups torn Romaine lettuce leaves

8 ounces cooked boneless lean roast beef, thinly sliced

2 small oranges, peeled and cut into thin wedges

1 medium red onion, thinly sliced

2 tablespoons minced fresh cilantro

$^1/_2$ medium jalapeño pepper, seeded, deveined and minced, or to taste (wear gloves to prevent irritation)

2 tablespoons red wine vinegar

2 teaspoons vegetable oil

$^1/_2$ teaspoon salt

1 cup sliced cooked beets

1. To prepare salad, in medium bowl, combine lettuce, roast beef, oranges, onion, cilantro and pepper; set aside.
2. To prepare dressing, in small jar with tight-fitting lid or small bowl, combine vinegar, oil and salt; cover and shake well or, with wire whisk, blend until combined.
3. Pour dressing over salad; toss to combine.
4. Arrange $^1/_4$ cup beets on each of 4 salad plates; top each with an equal amount of salad mixture.

Serving (1$^1/_2$ cups) provides: $^1/_2$ Fat, $^1/_2$ Fruit, 3 Vegetables, 2 Proteins.

Per serving: 187 Calories, 6 g Total Fat, 2 g Saturated Fat, 46 mg Cholesterol, 338 mg Sodium, 14 g Total Carbohydrate, 4 g Dietary Fiber, 18 g Protein, 63 mg Calcium.

HUNGARIAN GOULASH SOUP

Makes 4 servings

Although often thought of as a heavy stew, traditional goulash is actually a rich, robust soup like this one. For a simple dinner, serve it with egg noodles.

1 teaspoon vegetable oil	1 tablespoon paprika
2 medium onions, chopped	1 bay leaf
10 ounces boneless lean beef loin or round, cut into $^3/_4$" cubes	1 medium carrot, cut into $^3/_4$" chunks
1 tablespoon all-purpose flour	5 ounces all-purpose potato, pared and cubed
2 cups low-sodium beef broth	
2 tablespoons red wine vinegar	

1. In large pot or Dutch oven, heat oil; add onions. Cook over medium heat, stirring frequently, 3–5 minutes, until onions are softened. Add beef; cook, stirring frequently, 4–5 minutes, until browned on all sides and cooked through. Sprinkle beef mixture with flour; cook, stirring constantly, 1 minute, until evenly coated (do not burn).
2. Add broth, vinegar, paprika, bay leaf and 1 cup water to beef mixture; bring liquid to a boil. Reduce heat to low; simmer, covered, stirring occasionally, 1–1$^1/_2$ hours, until beef is tender.
3. Add carrot and potato to beef mixture; simmer, stirring occasionally, 30 minutes, until beef and vegetables are very tender. Remove and discard bay leaf. Divide evenly among 4 bowls and serve.

Serving (1 cup) provides: $^1/_4$ Fat, 1 Vegetable, 2 Proteins, $^1/_4$ Bread, 20 Optional Calories.

Per serving: 190 Calories, 6 g Total Fat, 2 g Saturated Fat, 42 mg Cholesterol, 90 mg Sodium, 15 g Total Carbohydrate, 2 g Dietary Fiber, 20 g Protein, 27 mg Calcium.

CHILI-BEEF SOUP

Makes 4 servings

This satisfying soup freezes well, so make a double batch! Divide the leftovers into serving-size portions and freeze, then defrost and heat for a quick, satisfying meal. For a hearty winter supper, serve the chili topped with hot red pepper sauce, minced fresh cilantro, scallions or jalapeño pepper, nonfat sour cream or grated cheese, along with sides of corn bread and a green salad.

1 teaspoon vegetable oil
4 medium onions, diced
¹/₂ medium red bell pepper, diced
¹/₂ medium green bell pepper, diced
10 ounces boneless lean beef loin or round, cut into ¹/₂" cubes*
1 medium carrot, diced
3 tablespoons mild or hot chili powder
1 large garlic clove, minced

8 ounces drained cooked red kidney, pinto or black beans
1¹/₂ cups low-sodium beef broth
1 cup canned whole Italian tomatoes (no salt added), chopped (reserve juice)
1 teaspoon dried oregano
¹/₄ teaspoon cinnamon
¹/₄ teaspoon salt
¹/₄ teaspoon freshly ground black pepper
1 tablespoon fine yellow cornmeal

1. In large nonstick saucepan, heat oil; add onions and red and green bell peppers. Cook over medium heat, stirring frequently, 8–10 minutes, until onions are golden brown. Remove onion mixture from saucepan; set aside.
2. In same saucepan, cook beef over medium heat, stirring frequently, 8–10 minutes, until browned on all sides and cooked through.
3. Reduce heat to low; add carrot, chili powder and garlic. Cook, stirring constantly, 2 minutes, until beef and carrot are evenly coated (do not burn).
4. Add beans, broth, tomatoes with juice, oregano, cinnamon, salt, black pepper and onion mixture to beef mixture; bring liquid to a boil. Reduce heat to low; simmer, covered, stirring occasionally, 1¹/₂–2 hours, until beef is very tender.
5. In small bowl, combine cornmeal and 3 tablespoons cold water; stir into beef mixture. Simmer, uncovered, 15 minutes, stirring frequently, until soup is slightly thickened. Divide evenly among 4 bowls and serve.

If you prefer starting with cooked meat, substitute 8 ounces cooked boneless beef steak, roast beef or roast pork, cut into ¹/₂" cubes; omit step 2 and cook meat with the carrot, garlic and chili powder.

Serving (1¹/₂ cups) provides: ¹/₄ Fat, 2¹/₂ Vegetables, 3 Proteins, 20 Optional Calories.

Per serving: 280 Calories, 7 g Total Fat, 2 g Saturated Fat, 42 mg Cholesterol, 371 mg Sodium, 32 g Total Carbohydrate, 7 g Dietary Fiber, 25 g Protein, 88 mg Calcium.

BORSCHT

Makes 4 servings

Although recipes vary, traditionally borscht does have meat in it. This version has the rich flavor of meat, along with the sweetness of beets.

1 teaspoon vegetable oil	1 bay leaf
2 medium onions, chopped	1 garlic clove, minced
10 ounces boneless lean beef or pork loin, cut into ¹/₂" cubes	¹/₂ teaspoon salt
4 cups low-sodium beef broth	2 cups chopped green cabbage
2 cups shredded pared trimmed beets	¹/₄ cup tomato paste (no salt)
	¹/₄ cup nonfat sour cream
	¹/₄ cup minced fresh dill

1. In large pot or Dutch oven, heat oil; add onions. Cook over medium heat, stirring frequently, 3–5 minutes, until onions are softened. Remove onion mixture from pot; set aside.
2. In same pot, cook beef, stirring frequently, 4–5 minutes, until browned on all sides and cooked through. Add broth, beets, bay leaf, garlic, salt, 2 cups water and reserved onion mixture; bring liquid to a boil. Reduce heat to low; simmer, stirring occasionally, 45–55 minutes, until beef is tender.
3. Add cabbage and tomato paste to beef mixture; cook, stirring occasionally, 20 minutes, until cabbage is tender. Remove and discard bay leaf.
4. Divide soup evenly among 4 bowls. Spoon 1 tablespoon sour cream onto each portion; sprinkle each with 1 tablespoon dill.

Serving (1¹/₃ cups) provides: ¹/₄ Fat, 3 Vegetables, 2 Proteins, 30 Optional Calories.

Per serving: 213 Calories, 5 g Total Fat, 2 g Saturated Fat, 42 mg Cholesterol, 464 mg Sodium, 17 g Total Carbohydrate, 3 g Dietary Fiber, 24 g Protein, 83 mg Calcium.

BELGIAN BEEF WITH BEER

Makes 4 servings

If you like onions, you'll love this rich stew. Serve it with noodles or boiled potatoes and, of course, beer.

2 teaspoons vegetable oil
4 medium onions, thinly sliced
1 large garlic clove, minced
2 tablespoons all-purpose flour
1/2 teaspoon salt
1/4 teaspoon freshly ground
   black pepper
15 ounces boneless lean beef loin
   or round, cut into 2" cubes

12 fluid ounces dark beer
1/2 cup low-sodium beef broth
1 teaspoon firmly packed dark
   brown sugar
1 bay leaf
1 teaspoon cider vinegar
1/4 teaspoon dried thyme leaves

1. In large nonstick skillet, heat 1 teaspoon of the oil; add onions. Cook over medium heat, stirring frequently, 8–10 minutes, until onions are golden brown. Stir in garlic; cook, stirring frequently, 2 minutes. With slotted spoon, remove onion mixture from skillet; set aside.
2. On sheet of wax paper or paper plate, combine flour, salt and pepper; add beef, turning to coat evenly. Set remaining flour mixture aside.
3. In same skillet, heat remaining 1 teaspoon oil; add beef. Cook over medium heat, stirring frequently, 8–10 minutes, until beef is browned on all sides and cooked through. Add beer, broth, brown sugar, bay leaf, vinegar and thyme; bring liquid to a boil, scraping up browned bits from bottom of skillet. Return onions to mixture. Reduce heat to low; simmer, covered, stirring occasionally, 1 1/2–2 hours, until beef is very tender.
4. In cup or small bowl, combine remaining flour mixture and 2 tablespoons cold water, stirring until flour is dissolved. Stir dissolved flour into beef mixture; simmer, uncovered, stirring frequently, 10 minutes, until mixture is slightly thickened. Remove and discard bay leaf. Divide evenly among 4 bowls and serve.

Serving (1 1/2 cups) provides: 1/2 Fat, 1 Vegetable, 3 Proteins, 60 Optional Calories.

Per serving: 264 Calories, 8 g Total Fat, 3 g Saturated Fat, 63 mg Cholesterol, 353 mg Sodium, 15 g Total Carbohydrate, 2 g Dietary Fiber, 25 g Protein, 36 mg Calcium.

GOULASH

Makes 4 servings

This brightly colored classic goes well with noodles or rice, or boiled potatoes. To achieve the most authentic color and flavor, be sure to use authentic Hungarian paprika, now widely available in supermarkets.

2 teaspoons vegetable oil
3 medium onions, thinly sliced
4 large garlic cloves, minced
15 ounces boneless lean beef loin
   or round, cut into 2" cubes

2 tablespoons mild or 1 teaspoon
   hot Hungarian paprika
2 cups tomato sauce (no salt added)
1 cup low-sodium beef broth
$^1/_2$ teaspoon dried thyme leaves

1. In large nonstick skillet, heat 1 teaspoon of the oil; add onions. Cook over medium heat, stirring frequently, 8–10 minutes, until onions are golden brown. Stir in garlic; cook, stirring frequently, 2 minutes. With slotted spoon, remove onion mixture from skillet; set aside.
2. In same skillet, heat remaining 1 teaspoon oil; add beef. Cook over medium heat, stirring frequently, 8–10 minutes, until beef is browned on all sides and cooked through; reduce heat to low. Sprinkle beef with paprika; cook, stirring constantly, 2–3 minutes, until beef is evenly coated (do not burn).
3. Add tomato sauce, broth, thyme and reserved onion mixture to beef mixture; bring liquid to a boil, scraping up browned bits from bottom of skillet. Reduce heat to low; simmer, covered, stirring occasionally, $1^1/_2$–2 hours, until beef is very tender. Divide evenly among 4 plates and serve.

Serving (1 cup) provides: $^1/_2$ Fat, $2^3/_4$ Vegetables, 3 Proteins, 5 Optional Calories.

Per serving: 255 Calories, 9 g Total Fat, 3 g Saturated Fat, 63 mg Cholesterol, 109 mg Sodium, 17 g Total Carbohydrate, 3 g Dietary Fiber, 27 g Protein, 33 mg Calcium.

COUNTRY-STYLE BEEF STEW

Makes 8 servings

Stews make great do-ahead meals; when you have the time, prepare them, then divide into serving-size portions and freeze, covered, for up to 2 months. To serve, simply thaw and heat.

15 ounces boneless lean beef loin or round, cut into 2" cubes

2 cups tomato sauce (no salt added)

1 cup low-sodium beef broth

2 fluid ounces ($^1/_4$ cup) dry red wine

1 tablespoon Worcestershire sauce

1 bay leaf

1 teaspoon dried thyme leaves

1 teaspoon dried rosemary leaves, crumbled

1 teaspoon dried marjoram

1 large garlic clove, crushed

$^1/_2$ teaspoon freshly ground black pepper

2 medium carrots, thinly sliced

10 ounces all-purpose potatoes, pared and diced

1 medium onion, diced

$^1/_2$ cup thinly sliced mushrooms

1 medium celery stalk, thinly sliced

1 cup fresh or thawed frozen green peas

1. Spray medium nonstick saucepan with nonstick cooking spray; heat. Add beef; cook over medium heat, stirring frequently, 8–10 minutes, until beef is browned on all sides and cooked through. Stir in tomato sauce, broth, wine, Worcestershire sauce, bay leaf, thyme, rosemary, marjoram, garlic and pepper; bring liquid to a boil. Reduce heat to low; simmer, covered, stirring occasionally, 1–1$^1/_2$ hours, until beef is tender.

2. Stir carrots, potatoes, onion, mushrooms and celery into beef mixture; simmer, covered, stirring occasionally, 30 minutes, until vegetables and beef are very tender. Stir in peas; simmer 10 minutes, until peas are tender. Remove and discard bay leaf. Divide evenly among 4 plates and serve.

Serving (1 cup) provides: 1$^3/_4$ Vegetables, 1$^1/_2$ Proteins, $^1/_2$ Bread, 10 Optional Calories.

Per serving: 169 Calories, 3 g Total Fat, 1 g Saturated Fat, 31 mg Cholesterol, 89 mg Sodium, 18 g Total Carbohydrate, 3 g Dietary Fiber, 15 g Protein, 30 mg Calcium.

BEEF STEW WITH SPRING VEGETABLES

Makes 4 servings

Vary this delicately flavored, unthickened stew by adding whatever young spring vegetables are in the marketplace; use anything *except* beets (their red color bleeds and will spoil the attractive colors of the stew).

1 teaspoon olive oil	2 cups cut green beans
2 cups pearl onions	2 tablespoons minced fresh
2 cups baby carrots	flat-leaf parsley
2 medium leeks, well-washed and	2 tablespoons minced
thinly sliced	fresh dill
15 ounces boneless lean beef loin	1 teaspoon grated lemon zest*
or round, cut into 2" cubes	1 tablespoon fresh lemon juice,
1 cup low-sodium beef broth	or to taste
1 cup low-sodium chicken broth	$^{1}/_{4}$ teaspoon freshly ground
1 pound 4 ounces tiny new	black pepper
potatoes	

1. In large nonstick saucepan, heat oil; add onions, carrots and leeks. Cook over medium heat, stirring frequently, 6–7 minutes, until onions are lightly browned. Remove vegetable mixture from saucepan; set aside.
2. In same saucepan, cook beef over medium heat, stirring frequently, 8–10 minutes, until beef is browned on all sides and cooked through. Add beef and chicken broths; bring liquid to a boil. Reduce heat to low; simmer, covered, stirring occasionally, 1–1$^{1}/_{2}$ hours, until beef is tender.
3. Add potatoes, green beans and reserved vegetable mixture to beef mixture; simmer, covered, 15–20 minutes, until vegetables and beef are very tender.
4. Stir in parsley, dill, zest, juice and pepper. Divide evenly among 4 bowls and serve.

Serving (1$^{1}/_{2}$ cups) provides: $^{1}/_{4}$ Fat, 4 Vegetables, 3 Proteins, 1 Bread, 10 Optional Calories.

Per serving: 395 Calories, 8 g Total Fat, 3 g Saturated Fat, 63 mg Cholesterol, 163 mg Sodium, 51 g Total Carbohydrate, 6 g Dietary Fiber, 31 g Protein, 119 mg Calcium.

---

   * *The zest of the lemon is the peel without any of the pith (white membrane). To remove zest from lemon, use a zester or the fine side of a vegetable grater.*

BURGUNDY BEEF STEW

Makes 4 servings

Serve this fragrant, savory classic with the best crusty bread you can find, a green salad and a glass of dry red wine.

4 cups whole small mushrooms, woody ends trimmed
2 cups pearl onions
1 medium onion, minced
1 large garlic clove, minced
15 ounces boneless lean beef loin or round, cut into 2" cubes
8 fluid ounces (1 cup) dry red wine
1 cup low-sodium beef broth

2 slices crisp-cooked bacon, crumbled
1 bay leaf
$1/2$ teaspoon dried rosemary leaves, crumbled
$1/4$ teaspoon dried thyme leaves
$1/4$ teaspoon freshly ground black pepper
Pinch ground nutmeg
2 teaspoons all-purpose flour

1. In large nonstick saucepan, combine mushrooms, pearl onions, minced onion and garlic; cook over medium heat, stirring frequently, 8–10 minutes, until minced onion is golden brown. Remove vegetable mixture from saucepan; set aside.
2. In same saucepan, cook beef over medium heat, stirring frequently, 8–10 minutes, until browned on all sides and cooked through. Add wine, broth, bacon, bay leaf, rosemary, thyme, pepper and nutmeg; bring liquid to a boil. Reduce heat to low; simmer, covered, stirring occasionally, $1^1/2$–2 hours, until beef is very tender.
3. Add reserved vegetables to beef mixture; simmer, covered, 10 minutes, until mixture is heated through.
4. In small bowl, combine flour and $1/4$ cup cold water, stirring until flour is dissolved. Stir dissolved flour into beef mixture; simmer, uncovered, stirring frequently, 10–15 minutes, until vegetables are tender and mixture is slightly thickened. Remove and discard bay leaf. Divide evenly among 4 bowls and serve.

Serving ($1^1/4$ cups) provides: $3^1/4$ Vegetables, 3 Proteins, 80 Optional Calories.

Per serving: 284 Calories, 8 g Total Fat, 3 g Saturated Fat, 65 mg Cholesterol, 146 mg Sodium, 16 g Total Carbohydrate, 2 g Dietary Fiber, 28 g Protein, 60 mg Calcium.

SAUERBRATEN STEW

Makes 4 servings

$^3/_4$ cup red wine vinegar
1 bay leaf
6 whole black peppercorns
6 juniper berries*
3 whole cloves
15 ounces boneless lean beef loin
    or round, cut into 2" cubes
2 medium onions, thinly sliced
1 medium carrot, sliced

1 medium leek, well-washed
    and sliced
$^1/_2$ cup parsnip, sliced
1 teaspoon vegetable oil
8 fluid ounces (1 cup) dry red wine
1 packet low-sodium instant
    beef broth and seasoning mix
3 gingersnap cookies, finely
    crushed

1. To prepare marinade, in gallon-size sealable plastic bag, combine vinegar, bay leaf, peppercorns, juniper berries and cloves; add beef, onions, carrot, leek and parsnip. Seal bag, squeezing out air; turn to coat beef and vegetables. Refrigerate at least 8 hours or up to 2 days, turning bag occasionally.
2. Remove beef from marinade; pat dry with paper towels. Reserve vegetables and marinade.
3. In medium nonstick saucepan, heat oil; add beef. Cook over medium heat, stirring frequently, 8–10 minutes, until beef is browned on all sides and cooked through. Add wine, broth mix and reserved vegetables and marinade; bring liquid to a boil. Reduce heat to low; simmer, covered, stirring occasionally, $1^1/_2$–2 hours, until beef is very tender.
4. With slotted spoon, transfer beef and vegetables to serving platter; cover to keep warm. Remove and discard bay leaf and cloves from liquid remaining in saucepan. Remove peppercorns and juniper berries; crush and return to saucepan.
5. With wire whisk, stir gingersnaps into liquid; continuing to stir, cook over medium heat 5 minutes, until mixture is slightly thickened. Spoon sauce over warm beef and vegetables, divide evenly among 4 plates and serve.

Serving ($1^1/_2$ cups) provides: $^1/_4$ Fat, $1^1/_2$ Vegetables, 3 Proteins, $^1/_4$ Bread, 75 Optional Calories.

Per serving: 291 Calories, 8 g Total Fat, 2 g Saturated Fat, 63 mg Cholesterol, 118 mg Sodium, 20 g Total Carbohydrate, 3 g Dietary Fiber, 25 g Protein, 53 mg Calcium.

Juniper berries are available in the seasonings section of most gourmet food stores and some supermarkets.

DAUBE DE BOEUF

Makes 4 servings

This rich, savory stew gets a flavor boost from parsley, mustard, capers and garlic added just before serving. It is one of the few stews that tastes as good served at room temperature as it does right from the oven.

4 juniper berries*
8 fluid ounces (1 cup) dry white wine
1 bay leaf
$^1/_2$ teaspoon dried thyme leaves
$^1/_4$ teaspoon dried marjoram
$^1/_4$ teaspoon freshly ground black pepper
15 ounces boneless lean beef loin or round, cut into 2" cubes
3 cups whole small mushrooms, woody ends trimmed

2 medium carrots, sliced
2 medium onions, sliced
2 teaspoons all-purpose flour
$^1/_2$ cup low-sodium beef broth
2 tablespoons minced fresh flat-leaf parsley
2 tablespoons Dijon-style mustard
2 teaspoons rinsed drained capers, finely chopped
2 garlic cloves, minced

1. To prepare marinade, place juniper berries into heat-resistant cup or small bowl; add hot water to cover. Let stand 30 minutes; drain, discarding liquid.
2. Crush soaked berries. In gallon-size sealable plastic bag, combine wine, bay leaf, thyme, marjoram, pepper and crushed juniper berries; add beef, mushrooms, carrots and onions. Seal bag, squeezing out air; turn to coat beef and vegetables. Refrigerate overnight, turning bag occasionally.
3. Preheat oven to 300° F. Spray 2-quart flameproof casserole with nonstick cooking spray.
4. Remove beef from marinade; pat dry with paper towels. Reserve vegetables and marinade.
5. Place flour onto sheet of wax paper or paper plate; add beef, turning to coat evenly.
6. With slotted spoon, transfer one third of the marinated vegetables to prepared casserole; top with half of the beef. Repeat layers; top with remaining vegetables. Pour marinade and broth over beef mixture; add enough water until liquid comes halfway up sides of casserole. Place casserole over medium-high heat; bring liquid just to a boil. Remove from heat; bake, covered, $1^1/_2$–2 hours, until beef is very tender.

7. In small bowl, combine parsley, mustard, capers and garlic; stir into beef mixture. Let stand 5 minutes, until flavors are blended. Remove and discard bay leaf. Divide evenly among 4 bowls and serve.

Serving (1¹/₂ cups) provides: 3 Vegetables, 3 Proteins, 60 Optional Calories.

Per serving: 263 Calories, 7 g Total Fat, 2 g Saturated Fat, 63 mg Cholesterol, 313 mg Sodium, 14 g Total Carbohydrate, 3 g Dietary Fiber, 26 g Protein, 47 mg Calcium.

* Juniper berries are available in the seasonings section of most gourmet food stores and some supermarkets.

BOLIVIAN BEEF STEW

Makes 4 servings

There are many variations of this dish, some of which include chicken or fish. Adjust the degree of heat to suit your taste; serve with a crisp green salad and hot corn muffins.

1 teaspoon vegetable oil
4 medium onions, chopped
$^1/_2$ medium red or green bell pepper, chopped
1 medium jalapeño pepper, seeded, deveined and chopped, or to taste (wear gloves to prevent irritation)
15 ounces boneless lean beef loin or round, cut into 2" cubes
2 cups canned whole Italian tomatoes (no salt added), chopped (reserve juice)

1 cup low-sodium beef broth
$^1/_4$ teaspoon salt
2 cups diced pared acorn or other winter squash
10 ounces diced pared red potatoes
Two 5" ears of corn, cut into 1" pieces
2 tablespoons minced fresh cilantro, to garnish

1. In medium nonstick saucepan, heat oil; add onions and bell and jalapeño peppers. Cook over medium heat, stirring frequently, 6–7 minutes, until onions are lightly browned. Remove onion mixture from saucepan; set aside.
2. In same saucepan, cook beef over medium heat, stirring frequently, 8–10 minutes, until beef is browned on all sides and cooked through. Add tomatoes with juice, broth, salt and reserved onion mixture; bring liquid to a boil. Reduce heat to low; simmer, covered, stirring occasionally, 1–1$^1/_2$ hours, until beef is tender.
3. Add squash, potatoes and corn to beef mixture; simmer, covered, 20 minutes, until vegetables and beef are very tender. Divide evenly among 4 bowls, sprinkle with cilantro and serve.

Serving (1$^1/_2$ cups) provides: $^1/_4$ Fat, 2$^1/_2$ Vegetables, 3 Proteins, 1$^1/_2$ Breads, 5 Optional Calories.

Per serving: 337 Calories, 8 g Total Fat, 3 g Saturated Fat, 63 mg Cholesterol, 428 mg Sodium, 38 g Total Carbohydrate, 6 g Dietary Fiber, 30 g Protein, 75 mg Calcium.

African Beef and Plantain Stew

Makes 4 servings

Plantains are banana-like vegetables that get creamy as they cook and add a hint of sweetness to this filling stew.

$^1/_2$ teaspoon vegetable oil
4 medium onions, sliced
4 large garlic cloves, minced
12 ounces boneless lean beef loin or round, cut into 2" cubes
1 cup low-sodium beef broth
$^1/_2$ cup stewed tomatoes (no salt added), chopped
$^1/_2$ teaspoon crushed red pepper flakes, or to taste

3 tablespoons peanut butter
1 cup sliced peeled yellow-ripe plantain, pared and cut into $^1/_2$" slices
1 cup diced pared acorn or other winter squash
2 tablespoons fresh lemon juice
$^1/_2$ ounce unsalted shelled peanuts, chopped, to garnish

1. In large nonstick skillet, heat oil; add onions. Cook over medium heat, stirring frequently, 8–10 minutes, until onions are golden brown. Add garlic; cook, stirring frequently, 2 minutes. Remove onion mixture from skillet; set aside.
2. Spray same skillet with nonstick cooking spray; heat. Add beef; cook over medium heat, stirring frequently, 8–10 minutes, until beef is browned on all sides and cooked through. Add broth, tomatoes, pepper flakes and reserved onion mixture; cook, scraping up brown bits from bottom of skillet, 5 minutes, until heated through and well-combined. Reduce heat to low; simmer, covered, stirring occasionally, 1–1$^1/_2$ hours, until beef is tender.
3. In blender or food processor, combine $^1/_2$ cup liquid from skillet and peanut butter; let stand until slightly cooled, then purée until smooth. Transfer peanut butter mixture to beef mixture; stir to combine. Stir in plantain and squash; simmer, covered, stirring frequently, 30 minutes, until plantain and squash are tender and beef is very tender. Stir in juice; divide evenly among 4 bowls, sprinkle with peanuts and serve.

Serving (1$^1/_2$ cups) provides: 1 Fat, 1$^1/_4$ Vegetables, 3 Proteins, $^3/_4$ Bread, 20 Optional Calories.

Per serving: 339 Calories, 14 g Total Fat, 3 g Saturated Fat, 50 mg Cholesterol, 212 mg Sodium, 31 g Total Carbohydrate, 4 g Dietary Fiber, 26 g Protein, 59 mg Calcium.

GREEK BEEF STEW

Makes 4 servings

This fragrant, colorful stew should be cooked until the beef is meltingly tender; serve it with boiled new potatoes or over your favorite pasta.

2 teaspoons vegetable oil	1 tablespoon red wine vinegar
2 cups pearl onions	1 large bay leaf
15 ounces boneless lean beef loin or round, cut into 2" cubes	$^1/_2$ teaspoon salt
	$^1/_2$ teaspoon cinnamon
$1^1/_2$ cups canned tomato purée (no salt added)	$^1/_4$ teaspoon freshly ground black pepper
2 fluid ounces ($^1/_4$ cup) dry red wine	$^1/_4$ teaspoon dried rosemary leaves, crumbled

1. In large nonstick skillet, heat 1 teaspoon of the oil; add onions. Cook over medium heat, stirring frequently, 8–10 minutes, until onions are golden brown. Remove onions from skillet; set aside.
2. In same skillet, heat remaining 1 teaspoon oil; add beef. Cook over medium heat, stirring frequently, 8–10 minutes, until beef is browned on all sides and cooked through.
3. Add tomato purée, wine, vinegar, bay leaf, salt, cinnamon, pepper, rosemary and reserved onions to browned beef; bring liquid to a boil, scraping up browned bits from bottom of skillet. Reduce heat to low; simmer, covered, stirring occasionally, adding 1 tablespoon water at a time if mixture begins to stick to skillet, $1^1/_2$–2 hours, until beef is very tender. Remove and discard bay leaf. Divide evenly among 4 bowls and serve.

Serving (1 cup) provides: $^1/_2$ Fat, $2^1/_2$ Vegetables, 3 Proteins, 15 Optional Calories.

Per serving: 256 Calories, 8 g Total Fat, 3 g Saturated Fat, 63 mg Cholesterol, 720 mg Sodium, 18 g Total Carbohydrate, 2 g Dietary Fiber, 25 g Protein, 64 mg Calcium.

BEEF WITH ADOBO SAUCE

Makes 4 servings

Find canned *chipotles en adobo,* smoked dried jalapeño peppers in a spicy sauce, in Latino groceries or some supermarkets. The peppers and sauce can be pureed, frozen in ice cube trays and then stored in bags in the freezer. Add a cube to soups, sauces or chili for a terrific flavor boost. Use it judiciously; it's *very* hot!

1 teaspoon vegetable oil
4 medium onions, sliced
2 garlic cloves, minced
15 ounces boneless lean beef loin
   or round, cut into 2" cubes
2 cups low-sodium beef broth
1 teaspoon pureed canned
   chipotles en adobo, or to taste
1 large or 2 small plum tomatoes,
   finely diced

2 medium scallions, sliced
1 medium jalapeño pepper,
   seeded, deveined and minced,
   or to taste (wear gloves to
   prevent irritation)
2 tablespoons minced fresh
   cilantro
2 teaspoons cornstarch, dissolved
   in 1 tablespoon water

1. In large nonstick skillet, heat ¹/₂ teaspoon of the oil; add onions. Cook over medium heat, stirring frequently, 15 minutes, until onions are deep golden brown. Add garlic; cook, stirring frequently, 2 minutes. Remove onion mixture from skillet; set aside.
2. In same skillet, heat remaining ¹/₂ teaspoon oil; add beef. Cook over medium heat, stirring frequently, 8–10 minutes, until beef is browned on all sides and cooked through. Add broth, chipotles, ¹/₂ cup water and reserved onion mixture; bring liquid to a boil. Reduce heat to low; simmer, covered, 1¹/₂–2 hours, until beef is very tender.
3. Meanwhile, in small bowl, combine tomato, scallions, jalapeño pepper and cilantro; set aside.
4. Stir dissolved cornstarch into beef mixture; simmer, uncovered, stirring constantly, 3 minutes, until liquid is slightly thickened. Divide evenly among 4 bowls, sprinkle with tomato mixture and serve.

Serving (1¹/₄ cups) provides: ¹/₄ Fat, 1¹/₂ Vegetables, 3 Proteins, 15 Optional Calories.

Per serving: 217 Calories, 7 g Total Fat, 2 g Saturated Fat, 63 mg Cholesterol, 114 mg Sodium, 10 g Total Carbohydrate, 2 g Dietary Fiber, 27 g Protein, 30 mg Calcium.

MEXICAN STUFFED POBLANOS

Makes 4 servings

If you can't find large poblano chiles at your greengrocer or supermarket, medium bell peppers may be substituted. Although the bell peppers require no peeling, they lack the flavor of the poblanos. Serve this dish with cream-style corn and steamed broccoli.

8 large smooth-skinned poblano chiles
1 teaspoon corn oil
2 medium onions, minced
2 garlic cloves, minced
10 ounces boneless lean beef loin or round, cut into $1/2$" cubes
2 tablespoons mild or hot chili powder
$1/4$ teaspoon anise seed
Pinch cumin seed
Pinch ground cloves
Pinch cinnamon

1 cup low-sodium beef broth
1 cup cooked long-grain rice
$1/4$ cup raisins
6 large or 10 small pimiento-stuffed green olives, sliced
$1/4$ teaspoon salt
$1/2$ cup tomato sauce (no salt added)
$1^1/2$ ounces extra-sharp cheddar cheese, grated
1 tablespoon freshly grated Parmesan cheese

1. Preheat broiler. Line baking sheet or pie pan with foil.
2. Set chiles onto prepared baking sheet; broil 6" from heat, turning frequently with tongs, until skin is lightly charred on all sides. Transfer chiles to plastic or paper bag; seal bag. Let chiles stand 20 minutes to cool. Wearing surgical gloves, slit chiles lengthwise; carefully remove and discard stems, seeds and veins. Peel away as much skin as possible, leaving chile flesh intact.
3. Reduce oven temperature to 350° F. Spray shallow 2-quart baking dish with nonstick cooking spray.
4. In large nonstick skillet, heat oil; add onions and garlic. Cook over medium heat, stirring frequently, 6–7 minutes, until onions are lightly browned. Remove onion mixture from skillet; set aside.
5. In same skillet, cook beef over medium heat, stirring frequently, 5–6 minutes, until beef is browned on all sides and cooked through; reduce heat to low. Add chili powder, anise and cumin seeds, cloves and cinnamon; cook, stirring constantly, 5 minutes, until beef is deep brown.

6. Add broth, $^1/_4$ cup water and reserved onion mixture to beef mixture; bring liquid to a boil. Reduce heat to low; simmer, covered, stirring occasionally, 1 hour, until beef is very tender. Remove from heat; stir in rice, raisins, olives and salt.

7. Place chiles, skinned-side down, onto work surface; spoon an equal amount of beef mixture lengthwise along center of each chile. Fold sides of chiles over filling to enclose; place, seam-side down, into prepared baking dish. Top stuffed chiles evenly with tomato sauce; sprinkle evenly with cheddar and Parmesan cheeses. Bake 40–45 minutes, until filling is heated through, cheese is browned and sauce is bubbling. Divide evenly among 4 plates and serve.

Serving (2 stuffed chiles with one-fourth of cheese and sauce) provides:
$^1/_2$ Fat, $^1/_2$ Fruit, 4 Vegetables, $2^1/_2$ Proteins, $^1/_2$ Bread, 15 Optional Calories.

Per serving: 383 Calories, 11 g Total Fat, 4 g Saturated Fat, 54 mg Cholesterol, 514 mg Sodium, 48 g Total Carbohydrate, 5 g Dietary Fiber, 27 g Protein, 170 mg Calcium.

TERIYAKI BEEF WITH MUSHROOMS AND CARAMELIZED ONIONS

Makes 4 servings

Caramelizing the onions brings out their sweetness and adds rich flavor and color to this quick dish. If you have all the ingredients ready before you begin cooking, this dish can be done by the time the rice is cooked.

2 teaspoons vegetable oil	³/₄ cup low-sodium beef broth
3 medium onions, thinly sliced	
3 cups thinly sliced mushrooms	2 tablespoons teriyaki sauce
2 garlic cloves, minced	1 tablespoon oyster sauce
1 teaspoon minced pared fresh ginger root	Pinch ground red pepper
	3 cups hot cooked long-grain rice
15 ounces boneless lean beef loin or round, cut into ¹/₄" strips	4 medium scallions, sliced

1. In large nonstick skillet, heat 1 teaspoon of the oil; add onions, mushrooms, garlic and ginger. Cook over medium heat, stirring frequently, 15 minutes, until onions are deep golden brown. Remove onion mixture from skillet; set aside.
2. In same skillet, heat remaining 1 teaspoon oil; add beef. Cook over medium heat, stirring frequently, 5–6 minutes, until beef is browned on all sides and cooked through. Remove beef from skillet; set aside.
3. In same skillet, combine broth, teriyaki and oyster sauces and pepper; bring liquid to a boil, scraping up browned bits from bottom of skillet. Reduce heat to low. Return onion mixture and beef to skillet; cook, stirring frequently, 2–3 minutes, until mixture is heated through.
4. Spoon rice onto serving platter; top with beef mixture. Serve sprinkled with scallions.

Serving (1 cup beef mixture with ³/₄ cup rice, 1 tablespoon scallions) provides: ¹/₂ Fat, 2¹/₂ Vegetables, 3 Proteins, 1¹/₂ Breads, 20 Optional Calories.

Per serving: 428 Calories, 9 g Total Fat, 3 g Saturated Fat, 63 mg Cholesterol, 608 mg Sodium, 54 g Total Carbohydrate, 2 g Dietary Fiber, 31 g Protein, 49 mg Calcium.

HEARTY HERBED MEATLOAF

Makes 6 servings

Meatloaf is always a favorite, and this one is sure to elicit cheers from the whole family; serve it with roasted root vegetables for a hearty and wholesome meal.

1¹/₂ teaspoons olive oil
3 medium carrots, diced
2 medium celery stalks, diced
1 medium onion, diced
2 garlic cloves, minced
10 ounces lean ground beef or combination of lean ground beef, pork and veal (10% or less fat)
1¹/₂ cups cooked long-grain rice

¹/₂ cup skim milk
3 egg whites
3 ounces boneless lean cooked ham, chopped
¹/₄ cup minced fresh flat-leaf parsley
1 teaspoon minced fresh rosemary leaves
¹/₂ teaspoon salt
¹/₂ teaspoon freshly ground black pepper

1. Preheat oven to 350° F. Spray 8 × 4" loaf pan with nonstick cooking spray.
2. In large nonstick skillet, heat oil; add carrots, celery and onion. Cook over medium heat, stirring frequently, 8–10 minutes, until onion is golden brown. Add garlic; cook, stirring frequently, 2 minutes. Remove from heat; let cool slightly.
3. In large bowl, combine beef, rice, milk, egg whites, ham, parsley, rosemary, salt, pepper and cooled vegetable mixture; transfer to prepared loaf pan, pressing down firmly. Bake 50–60 minutes, until meatloaf is firm and cooked through. Remove from oven; let stand 5 minutes. Cut into 6 equal slices and serve.

Serving (one-sixth of loaf) provides: ¹/₄ Fat, 1¹/₄ Vegetables, 2 Proteins, ¹/₂ Bread, 10 Optional Calories.

Per serving with beef: 266 Calories, 7 g Total Fat, 2 g Saturated Fat, 37 mg Cholesterol, 454 mg Sodium, 23 g Total Carbohydrate, 2 g Dietary Fiber, 17 g Protein, 61 mg Calcium.

Per serving with beef, pork and veal: 219 Calories, 6 g Total Fat, 2 g Saturated Fat, 41 mg Cholesterol, 455 mg Sodium, 23 g Total Carbohydrate, 2 g Dietary Fiber, 17 g Protein, 67 mg Calcium.

Meatloaf with Peppers and Gravy

Makes 8 servings

This home-style loaf is good served hot with mashed sweet potatoes, or cold as a filling for sandwiches. The combination of lean ground beef and poultry keeps the loaf lean, while the little bit of liver gives it a wonderful richness.

15 ounces lean ground beef (10% or less fat)	$^1/_4$ cup minced fresh flat-leaf parsley
14 ounces ground skinless turkey or chicken breast	2 large bay leaves, stems and center veins removed
$^1/_2$ cup + 1 tablespoon plain dried bread crumbs	1 large garlic clove, peeled
1 teaspoon dried oregano	2 teaspoons vegetable oil
1 teaspoon salt	1 medium celery stalk, minced
$^1/_2$ teaspoon freshly ground black pepper	$^1/_2$ medium red or yellow bell pepper, minced
2 medium carrots, minced	$^1/_4$ medium green bell pepper, minced
2 medium onions, minced	1 tablespoon + 2 teaspoons Worcestershire sauce
1 cup + 2 tablespoons tomato sauce (no salt added)	1 tablespoon all-purpose flour
2 ounces beef liver, diced	2 cups low-sodium beef broth

1. Preheat oven to 350° F. Spray 8 × 4" loaf pan with nonstick cooking spray.
2. To prepare meatloaf, in large bowl, combine beef, turkey, bread crumbs, oregano, salt and black pepper; set aside.
3. In blender or food processor, combine $^1/_2$ cup of the carrots, $^1/_2$ cup of the onions, $^3/_4$ cup of the tomato sauce, the liver, parsley, bay leaves and garlic; purée until smooth. Transfer vegetable purée to bowl with beef mixture; set aside.
4. In medium nonstick skillet, heat oil; add celery, red and green bell peppers, remaining carrots and remaining onions. Cook over medium heat, stirring frequently, 6–7 minutes, until onions are lightly browned; remove from heat. Transfer half the cooked vegetable mixture to bowl with beef mixture; set remaining vegetable mixture aside.
5. Thoroughly combine beef mixture, vegetable purée and half the cooked vegetable mixture in bowl; transfer to prepared loaf pan, pressing down firmly.

6. In cup or small bowl, combine 1 tablespoon of the Worcestershire sauce and 1 tablespoon of the remaining tomato sauce; spread over beef mixture. Bake 50–60 minutes, until meatloaf is firm and cooked through.

7. Meanwhile, to prepare gravy, sprinkle flour over reserved cooked vegetable mixture; stir to combine. Cook over low heat, stirring constantly, 5 minutes, until mixture is golden brown. Add broth, remaining $1/4$ cup + 1 tablespoon tomato sauce and remaining 2 teaspoons Worcestershire sauce; cook, stirring constantly, until thickened. Cover; cook, stirring occasionally, 5–10 minutes, until vegetables are very tender and flavors are blended.

8. Remove meatloaf from oven; let stand 5 minutes. Cut meatloaf into 8 equal slices; serve each slice with 2 tablespoons gravy.

Serving (1 slice meatloaf with 2 tablespoons gravy) provides: $1/4$ Fat, $1^1/2$ Vegetables, 3 Proteins, $1/4$ Bread, 20 Optional Calories.

Per serving: 242 Calories, 8 g Total Fat, 3 g Saturated Fat, 86 mg Cholesterol, 487 mg Sodium, 15 g Total Carbohydrate, 2 g Dietary Fiber, 28 g Protein, 42 mg Calcium.

MEATBALL SANDWICH

Makes 4 servings

This sandwich has all the hearty, beefy flavor of the deli version, but just a fraction of the fat.

2 medium onions, finely chopped
³/₄ teaspoon salt
8 ounces lean ground beef (10% or less fat)
¹/₄ cup minced fresh flat-leaf parsley
3 tablespoons plain dried bread crumbs
1 teaspoon dried Italian seasoning
¹/₄ teaspoon freshly ground black pepper

2 teaspoons olive oil
1 medium onion, sliced
1 medium green bell pepper, slivered
2 cups canned whole Italian tomatoes (no salt added), coarsely chopped (reserve juice)
¹/₂ cup packed fresh basil leaves, slivered
One 8-ounce loaf Italian bread

1. In small bowl, combine chopped onions and ¹/₂ teaspoon of the salt; let stand 30 minutes.
2. Line medium sieve with cheesecloth or paper towels; place over medium bowl. Spoon onion mixture into sieve; press with back of wooden spoon to extract as much liquid as possible. Reserve solids; discard liquid.
3. In medium bowl, combine strained onions, beef, parsley, bread crumbs, Italian seasoning, and black pepper; form into 16 equal meatballs.
4. Spray large nonstick skillet with nonstick cooking spray; heat. Add meatballs; cook over medium heat, turning as needed, 8–10 minutes, until browned on all sides and cooked through. Remove meatballs from skillet; set aside.
5. In same skillet, heat oil; add sliced onion and bell pepper. Cook over medium heat, stirring frequently, 8–10 minutes, until onion is golden brown. Add tomatoes with juice and remaining ¹/₄ teaspoon salt; bring liquid to a boil. Reduce heat to low; simmer, covered, stirring occasionally, 20 minutes, until tomato mixture is thickened. Add meatballs; simmer, uncovered, stirring occasionally, 5 minutes, until meatballs are heated through. Stir in basil.
6. Split bread lengthwise almost all the way through; spread open. With slotted spoon, remove meatballs and place evenly along bottom half of bread; top evenly with tomato mixture. Replace top half of bread to enclose; cut crosswise into 4 equal portions and serve.

Serving (one-fourth of loaf) provides: $^1/_2$ Fat, $2^1/_4$ Vegetables, $1^1/_2$ Proteins, $2\ ^1/_4$ Breads.

Per serving: 361 Calories, 11 g Total Fat, 3 g Saturated Fat, 35 mg Cholesterol, 885 mg Sodium, 48 g Total Carbohydrate, 5 g Dietary Fiber, 20 g Protein, 205 mg Calcium.

MEATBALL STEW

Makes 4 servings

To reduce the cooking time, use $^1/_2$ cup cooked long-grain rice instead of the uncooked rice. Proceed as directed, but simmer the stew only 20 minutes, until the carrots are tender. Serve over parsleyed egg noodles or additional cooked rice.

8 ounces lean ground beef
   (10% or less fat)
8 ounces ground skinless turkey
   breast
1 medium onion, minced
$^1/_4$ medium green bell pepper,
   minced
2 ounces uncooked long-grain
   rice
$^1/_4$ cup minced fresh flat-leaf
   parsley
$^1/_2$ teaspoon salt

$^1/_4$ teaspoon freshly ground
   black pepper
$^1/_4$ teaspoon dried thyme leaves
$^1/_4$ teaspoon dried marjoram
1 teaspoon vegetable oil
1 cup pearl onions
$1^1/_2$ cups tomato sauce
   (no salt added)
1 cup baby carrots
2 medium celery stalks, sliced
$^1/_4$ cup low-sodium beef broth
1 garlic clove, minced

1. In medium bowl, combine beef, turkey, minced onion, bell pepper, rice, parsley, salt, black pepper, thyme and marjoram; form into 12 equal meatballs. Set aside.
2. In large nonstick skillet, heat oil; add pearl onions. Cook over medium heat, stirring frequently, 8–10 minutes, until onions are golden brown. Stir in tomato sauce, carrots, celery, broth and garlic; bring liquid to a boil. Add meatballs in a single layer; spoon liquid over meatballs. Reduce heat to low; simmer, covered, basting once or twice with liquid, 45 minutes, until vegetables are tender and meatballs are cooked through. Divide evenly among 4 plates and serve.

Serving (3 meatballs with $^3/_4$ cup vegetable mixture) provides: $^1/_4$ Fat, $3^1/_4$ Vegetables, 3 Proteins, $^1/_2$ Bread.

Per serving: 294 Calories, 8 g Total Fat, 3 g Saturated Fat, 68 mg Cholesterol, 402 mg Sodium, 28 g Total Carbohydrate, 3 g Dietary Fiber, 29 g Protein, 50 mg Calcium.

MEATBALL STROGANOFF

Makes 4 servings

This version of the classic beef Stroganoff is light on your pocketbook as well as your waistline. Serve this easy and elegant entrée with wide noodles and a cucumber-dill salad.

15 ounces lean ground beef
   (10% or less fat)
1 medium onion, minced
1 tablespoon Dijon-style mustard
2 teaspoons rinsed drained
   capers, finely chopped
$^1/_4$ teaspoon salt
$^1/_2$ teaspoon freshly ground
   black pepper

1 teaspoon vegetable oil
2 medium onions, thinly sliced
$^3/_4$ cup low-sodium beef
   broth
2 teaspoons cornstarch,
   dissolved in 1 tablespoon
   cold water
$^1/_4$ cup nonfat sour cream
$^1/_2$ teaspoon dried tarragon

1. In medium bowl, combine beef, minced onion, mustard, capers, salt and $^1/_4$ teaspoon of the pepper; form into 12 equal meatballs. Set aside.
2. In medium nonstick skillet, heat oil; add sliced onions. Cook over medium heat, stirring frequently, 8–10 minutes, until onions are golden brown. Remove onions from skillet; set aside.
3. In same skillet, cook meatballs over medium heat, turning as needed, until browned on all sides. Add broth and sliced onions; bring liquid to a boil. Reduce heat to low; stir in dissolved cornstarch. Simmer, stirring gently, until liquid is slightly thickened. Cover skillet; simmer, stirring occasionally, 15 minutes, until meatballs are cooked through.
4. Remove meatball mixture from heat; with wire whisk, gently stir in sour cream, tarragon and remaining $^1/_4$ teaspoon pepper. Divide evenly among 4 plates and serve.

Serving (3 meatballs with $^1/_3$ cup sour cream mixture) provides: $^1/_4$ Fat, $^3/_4$ Vegetable, 3 Proteins, 20 Optional Calories.

Per serving: 240 Calories, 12 g Total Fat, 4 g Saturated Fat, 66 mg Cholesterol, 363 mg Sodium, 8 g Total Carbohydrate, 1 g Dietary Fiber, 24 g Protein, 36 mg Calcium.

ZITI-MEATBALL BAKE

Makes 4 servings

This twist on meatballs and spaghetti will become a family favorite.

6 ounces ziti

10 ounces lean ground beef
(10% or less fat)

2 medium onions, finely chopped

1 teaspoon dried Italian
seasoning

1 garlic clove, minced

$1/2$ teaspoon salt

$1/2$ teaspoon freshly ground
black pepper

2 teaspoons olive oil

$1^1/2$ cups tomato sauce
(no salt added)

One 10-ounce package thawed
frozen chopped spinach,
thoroughly drained and
squeezed dry

$1/4$ cup minced fresh basil

3 ounces part-skim mozzarella
cheese, grated

1. Preheat oven to 350° F.
2. In large pot of boiling water, cook ziti 10–12 minutes, until tender. Drain, discarding liquid; set ziti aside.
3. Meanwhile, in medium bowl, combine beef, onions, Italian seasoning, garlic, salt and pepper; form into 16 equal meatballs.
4. In large nonstick skillet, heat oil; add meatballs. Cook over medium heat, turning as needed, 8–10 minutes, until browned on all sides and cooked through. Remove from heat.
5. Add tomato sauce, spinach, basil, half of the cheese and the ziti to meatballs; stir to combine. Transfer meatball mixture to 9" square baking pan; sprinkle with remaining cheese. Bake, covered, 20 minutes, until mixture is heated through and cheese is melted; bake uncovered, 10 minutes, until cheese is lightly browned. Divide evenly among 4 plates and serve.

Serving ($1^1/2$ cups) provides: $1/2$ Fat, 3 Vegetables, 3 Proteins, 2 Breads.

Per serving: 422 Calories, 14 g Total Fat, 5 g Saturated Fat, 56 mg Cholesterol, 503 mg Sodium, 47 g Total Carbohydrate, 5 g Dietary Fiber, 29 g Protein, 260 mg Calcium.

MIDEAST BEEF "SAUSAGES" WITH CREAM SAUCE

Makes 4 servings

Grill these flavorful little logs in a wire basket over an outdoor barbecue grill. Make plenty; they're also good cold! Serve with couscous or rice pilaf.

1 ounce unsalted shelled pistachios or blanched almonds
¹/₂ cup low-sodium chicken broth
2 tablespoons + 1 teaspoon fresh lemon juice
¹/₄ teaspoon ground cardamom
Pinch ground saffron, dissolved in 2 teaspoons hot water
³/₄ cup nonfat cream cheese
13 ounces lean ground beef (10% or less fat)

1 medium onion, minced
2 ounces drained cooked chick-peas (garbanzo beans), mashed
3 tablespoons minced fresh cilantro
1 tablespoon grated pared fresh ginger root
¹/₂ teaspoon ground coriander
¹/₂ teaspoon mild or hot curry powder
¹/₂ teaspoon salt
¹/₄ teaspoon ground cumin

1. Preheat oven to 425° F. Spray nonstick baking sheet with nonstick cooking spray.
2. To prepare sauce, in small nonstick skillet, toast nuts over medium-low heat, stirring constantly, 4–5 minutes, until fragrant and lightly browned. Add broth, 1 teaspoon of the juice, the cardamom and dissolved saffron; bring liquid to a boil. Reduce heat to low; simmer, stirring frequently, 1 minute.
3. Transfer nut mixture to blender or food processor. Add cream cheese; purée until mixture is very smooth. Let stand 30 minutes, until flavors are blended.
4. Meanwhile, to prepare "sausages," in medium bowl, combine beef, onion, chick-peas, cilantro, ginger, coriander, curry powder, salt, cumin and remaining 2 tablespoons juice; form into 12 equal sausage-shaped logs. Place logs onto prepared baking sheet; bake 10 minutes, until cooked through. Divide evenly among 4 plates and serve with sauce.

Serving (3 sausages with ¹/₄ cup sauce) provides: ¹/₂ Fat, ¹/₄ Vegetable, 3 Proteins, 50 Optional Calories.

Per serving: 277 Calories, 14 g Total Fat, 4 g Saturated Fat, 62 mg Cholesterol, 559 mg Sodium, 12 g Total Carbohydrate, 2 g Dietary Fiber, 28 g Protein, 150 mg Calcium.

CHILI BURGERS

Makes 4 servings

Rather than spooning chili on top of the burger, this hot and spicy chili is stirred right into the beef mixture.

2 teaspoons vegetable oil
1 medium onion, chopped
2 tablespoons mild or hot chili
  powder
1 tablespoon dried oregano
2 teaspoons ground cumin
1/2 teaspoon ground ginger
1/4 teaspoon ground allspice

6 ounces drained cooked red
  kidney beans
12 ounces lean ground beef
  (10% or less fat)
1 teaspoon salt
1/2 teaspoon freshly ground
  black pepper
Four 1-ounce Kaiser rolls, split

1. Spray rack in broiler pan with nonstick cooking spray. Preheat broiler.
2. In medium nonstick skillet, heat oil; add onion. Cook over medium heat, stirring frequently, 3–5 minutes, until onion is softened. Add chili powder, oregano, cumin, ginger and allspice; cook, stirring frequently, 2 minutes, until well-blended and fragrant. Remove from heat.
3. Stir beans into onion mixture; with fork, mash beans until coarsely crushed.
4. In medium bowl, combine beef, salt, pepper and bean mixture; form into 4 equal patties. Place patties onto prepared rack in broiler pan; broil 4" from heat, turning once, 14 minutes, until cooked through.
5. Serve each burger on a roll.

Serving (1 chili burger) provides: 1/2 Fat, 1/4 Vegetable, 3 Proteins, 1 Bread.

Per serving: 331 Calories, 13 g Total Fat, 4 g Saturated Fat, 53 mg Cholesterol, 807 mg Sodium, 30 g Total Carbohydrate, 4 g Dietary Fiber, 25 g Protein, 86 mg Calcium.

LITTLE JOES

Makes 4 servings

Have plenty of napkins available when you feast on this variation of the more familiar Sloppy Joes; the mellow flavor of spinach, combined with nippy jalapeño pepper and Dijon-style mustard, will make this San Francisco specialty a favorite.

$^1/_2$ cup canned whole Italian tomatoes (no salt added), chopped (reserve juice)

1 tablespoon firmly packed light or dark brown sugar

1 tablespoon balsamic vinegar

15 ounces lean ground beef (10% or less fat)

2 medium onions, diced

$^1/_2$ cup chopped washed trimmed spinach

$^1/_2$ medium jalapeño pepper, seeded, deveined and minced, or to taste (wear gloves to prevent irritation)

1 teaspoon Dijon-style mustard

1 teaspoon cider vinegar

1 teaspoon granulated sugar

Four 1-ounce Kaiser rolls, split

1. In small bowl, combine tomatoes with juice, brown sugar and balsamic vinegar; set aside.
2. In large nonstick skillet, combine beef and onions; cook over medium heat, stirring to break up meat, 4–5 minutes, until beef is no longer pink.
3. Add spinach, pepper, mustard, cider vinegar, granulated sugar and reserved tomato mixture to beef mixture; stir to combine. Bring mixture to a boil. Reduce heat to low; simmer, stirring occasionally, 20–30 minutes, until mixture is thickened and flavors are blended.
4. Place one-fourth of the beef mixture in each roll and serve.

Serving (1 sandwich) provides: $1^1/_4$ Vegetables, 3 Proteins, 1 Bread, 15 Optional Calories.

Per serving: 308 Calories, 12 g Total Fat, 4 g Saturated Fat, 66 mg Cholesterol, 318 mg Sodium, 25 g Total Carbohydrate, 2 g Dietary Fiber, 25 g Protein, 53 mg Calcium.

SHEPHERD'S PIE

Makes 8 servings

1 pound 14 ounces Yukon gold
  potatoes, pared and sliced
$^1/_2$ cup nonfat sour cream
$^1/_4$ teaspoon salt
Pinch ground white pepper
15 ounces lean ground beef
  (10% or less fat)
$1^1/_2$ cups tomato sauce
  (no salt added)
1 packet low-sodium instant beef
  broth and seasoning mix

1 teaspoon minced fresh
  oregano, or $^1/_4$ teaspoon
  dried
Pinch ground red pepper
$^1/_2$ cup fresh or thawed frozen
  corn kernels
$^1/_2$ cup fresh or thawed frozen
  green peas
$^1/_2$ medium carrot, sliced

1. Preheat oven to 350° F. Spray $2^1/_2$-quart casserole with nonstick cooking spray.
2. To prepare potato topping, place potatoes into medium saucepan; add water to cover. Bring liquid to a boil; reduce heat to low. Simmer 15–20 minutes, until potatoes are tender. Drain potatoes, reserving liquid; transfer potatoes to medium bowl.
3. Add sour cream, salt and white pepper to potatoes; with potato masher or fork, mash potato mixture until fluffy and as smooth as possible, adding 1 tablespoon reserved potato liquid at a time if mixture is too thick. Set aside.
4. To prepare meat mixture, in large nonstick skillet, cook beef, stirring to break up meat, 4–5 minutes, until no longer pink. Stir in tomato sauce, broth mix, oregano and red pepper; cook, stirring constantly, 2 minutes, until mixture is heated through.
5. Spoon meat mixture into prepared casserole; top evenly with corn, peas and carrot. Spread potato mixture over vegetables; bake 35 minutes, until edges are golden brown. Remove from oven; let stand 5 minutes. Divide evenly among 8 plates and serve.

Serving (1 cup) provides: 1 Vegetable, $1^1/_2$ Proteins, 1 Bread, 10 Optional Calories.

Per serving: 223 Calories, 6 g Total Fat, 2 g Saturated Fat, 33 mg Cholesterol, 138 mg Sodium, 27 g Total Carbohydrate, 3 g Dietary Fiber, 15 g Protein, 24 mg Calcium.

TAMALE PIE

Makes 4 servings

2 teaspoons vegetable oil	1 teaspoon dried oregano
2 medium onions, chopped	$^1/_4$ teaspoon ground cloves
1 medium carrot, diced	$^1/_4$ teaspoon ground red pepper
2 garlic cloves, minced	3 ounces yellow cornmeal
10 ounces lean ground beef (10% or less fat)	1 teaspoon salt
	$1^1/_2$ ounces Monterey Jack cheese, grated
2 tablespoons + $1^1/_2$ teaspoons mild or hot chili powder	$^1/_4$ medium red bell pepper, finely chopped
2 teaspoons ground cumin	2 tablespoons minced fresh cilantro
2 cups canned whole Italian tomatoes (no salt added), coarsely chopped (reserve juice)	$^1/_2$ teaspoon freshly ground black pepper

1. Preheat oven to 350° F. Spray 9" square baking pan with nonstick cooking spray.
2. In large nonstick skillet, heat oil; add onions and carrot. Cook over medium heat, stirring frequently, 3–5 minutes, until onions are softened. Add garlic; cook, stirring frequently, 5 minutes, until onions are golden brown.
3. Add beef, chili powder and cumin to onion mixture; cook, stirring to break up meat, 4–5 minutes, until no longer pink. Add tomatoes with juice, oregano, cloves and red pepper; bring mixture to a boil. Reduce heat to low; simmer 18–20 minutes, until mixture is thickened.
4. Meanwhile, in medium nonstick saucepan, combine cornmeal, salt and 2 cups water. Stirring constantly with wire whisk, bring mixture to a boil over medium heat. Reduce heat to low; simmer, stirring frequently, 15 minutes, until mixture is very thick and pulls away from sides of saucepan. Remove from heat; set aside to cool slightly. Stir in cheese, bell pepper, cilantro and black pepper.
5. Spoon beef mixture into prepared baking pan; spread evenly with cornmeal mixture. Bake, uncovered, 40 minutes, until beef mixture is bubbling and topping is lightly browned. Divide evenly among 4 plates and serve.

Serving (one-fourth of pie) provides: $^1/_2$ Fat, $2^1/_4$ Vegetables, $2^1/_2$ Proteins, 1 Bread.

Per serving: 336 Calories, 15 g Total Fat, 5 g Saturated Fat, 55 mg Cholesterol, 914 mg Sodium, 32 g Total Carbohydrate, 5 g Dietary Fiber, 22 g Protein, 165 mg Calcium.

CHILI CON CARNE

Makes 4 servings

Although Mexican in origin, chili con carne has become a favorite of the rest of North America. This version is pure perfection.

2 teaspoons vegetable oil
2 medium onions, chopped
1 medium carrot, diced
2 garlic cloves, minced
10 ounces lean ground beef (10% or less fat)
2 tablespoons + 1¹/₂ teaspoons mild or hot chili powder
2 teaspoons ground cumin

2 cups canned whole Italian tomatoes (no salt added), coarsely chopped (reserve juice)
1 teaspoon dried oregano
¹/₄ teaspoon ground cloves
¹/₄ teaspoon ground red pepper
4 ounces drained cooked black beans

1. In large nonstick saucepan, heat oil; add onions and carrot. Cook over medium heat, stirring frequently, 3–5 minutes, until onions are softened. Add garlic; cook, stirring frequently, 5 minutes, until onions are golden brown.
2. Add beef, chili powder and cumin to onion mixture; cook, stirring to break up meat, 4–5 minutes, until no longer pink. Add tomatoes with juice, oregano, cloves and pepper; bring mixture to a boil. Reduce heat to low; simmer 18–20 minutes, until mixture is thickened. Stir in beans; simmer 2–3 minutes, until beans are heated. Divide evenly among 4 plates and serve.

Serving (one-fourth of chili) provides: ¹/₂ Fat, 2 Vegetables, 2¹/₂ Proteins.

Per serving: 252 Calories, 11 g Total Fat, 3 g Saturated Fat, 44 mg Cholesterol, 306 mg Sodium, 22 g Total Carbohydrate, 5 g Dietary Fiber, 20 g Protein, 86 mg Calcium.

TOSTADA SALAD

Makes 4 servings

Remember that wonderful salad with the crispy tortilla base you enjoyed at a Mexican restaurant? This one is just as tasty, but with less fat and fewer calories! It's packed with flavor and contrasting textures, and makes a wonderful meal in just a few minutes.

1 teaspoon vegetable oil
4 medium onions, diced
5 ounces lean ground beef
   (10% or less fat)
2 tablespoons mild or hot chili
   powder
2 cups canned whole Italian
   tomatoes (no salt added),
   coarsely chopped (reserve
   juice)

$^{1}/_{2}$ teaspoon salt
4 cups shredded iceberg lettuce
3 medium tomatoes, diced
8 ounces drained cooked
   black beans
8 ounces cooked all-purpose
   potatoes, diced
4 ounces diced pared avocado
2 tablespoons red wine vinegar
4 ounces nonfat tortilla chips

1. In large nonstick skillet, heat oil; add half of the onions. Cook over medium heat, stirring frequently, 3–5 minutes, until onions are softened. Add beef; cook, stirring to break up meat, 4–5 minutes, until no longer pink. Add chili powder; cook, stirring constantly, 1 minute, until mixture is thoroughly combined. Add tomatoes with juice and salt; cook, stirring frequently, 10 minutes, until mixture is thickened. Remove from heat; set aside.
2. In large bowl, combine lettuce, tomatoes, beans, potatoes, avocado and remaining onions. Sprinkle with vinegar; toss to combine.
3. Divide tortilla chips evenly among 4 plates. Top each portion of chips with one-fourth of the lettuce mixture, then one-fourth of the beef mixture.

Serving (1 ounce chips with 2 cups lettuce mixture, $^{1}/_{3}$ cup beef mixture) provides: $1^{1}/_{4}$ Fats, $5^{1}/_{2}$ Vegetables, 2 Proteins, $1^{1}/_{2}$ Breads.

Per serving: 453 Calories, 12 g Total Fat, 2 g Saturated Fat, 22 mg Cholesterol, 557 mg Sodium, 70 g Total Carbohydrate, 10 g Dietary Fiber, 21 g Protein, 207 mg Calcium.

NEW ENGLAND BOILED DINNER

Makes 8 servings

For a flavorful and beautiful accompaniment, serve this delicious winter dish with roasted beets and an assortment of mustards and vinegars.

One 2-pound lean corned beef
   brisket*
24 fluid ounces beer
2 bay leaves
2 teaspoons whole allspice
2 teaspoons whole black
   peppercorns
2 teaspoons coriander seeds
2 teaspoons mustard seeds
2 pounds 8 ounces tiny new
   potatoes, or red potatoes, cut
   into 1" chunks

8 medium carrots, cut into
   1" chunks
4 cups pearl onions
1 small head green cabbage,
   cored and cut into
   8 wedges
2 tablespoons minced fresh
   flat-leaf parsley, to garnish

1. In large pot or Dutch oven, combine beef brisket, beer, bay leaves, allspice, peppercorns and coriander and mustard seeds; add cold water to bring liquid 6" above beef. Bring liquid to a boil; with slotted spoon, skim off foam that accumulates on surface. Reduce heat to low; cook, continuing to skim off accumulated foam, 30 minutes (do not boil). Partially cover pot; cook 3 hours, until beef feels tender when pierced with fork. Transfer beef to cutting board; cover to keep warm.
2. Place medium sieve over medium bowl. Strain liquid through sieve, reserving liquid; discard solids. Let liquid stand 15–20 minutes, until fat accumulates on top; with paper towels or large spoon, remove fat. Return liquid to pot.
3. Add potatoes and carrots to liquid in pot; bring liquid just to a boil. Reduce heat to low; simmer, uncovered, 5 minutes. Add onions to potato mixture; simmer 5 minutes. Add cabbage to potato mixture; simmer 10 minutes, until vegetables are tender.
4. Meanwhile, thinly slice beef across the grain; arrange on serving platter.
5. With slotted spoon, carefully remove vegetables from liquid; discard liquid. Surround beef with vegetables. Serve, sprinkled with parsley.

* *A 2-pound corned beef brisket will yield about 1 pound cooked corned beef.*

Serving (2 ounces beef with 3 cups vegetables) provides: $4^1/_2$ Vegetables, 2 Proteins, 1 Bread, 40 Optional Calories.

Per serving: 266 Calories, 2 g Total Fat, 1 g Saturated Fat, 25 mg Cholesterol, 745 mg Sodium, 47 g Total Carbohydrate, 7 g Dietary Fiber, 17 g Protein, 90 mg Calcium.

ASIAN BEEF HASH

Makes 8 servings

Many people take the leftovers from the week's meals and throw them together to make hash. This version, with the fragrance of Asian cuisine, breathes life into the traditional beef, potato and chopped vegetable hash, and tastes even better if made a day in advance.

2 teaspoons oriental sesame oil
1 medium onion, chopped
2 garlic cloves, minced
2 teaspoons grated pared fresh
    ginger root
15 ounces lean ground beef
    (10% or less fat)
10 ounces chopped washed
    trimmed spinach

4 cups cooked brown rice
1 medium tomato, chopped
1 tablespoon reduced-sodium
    soy sauce
1 teaspoon rice wine vinegar
1 teaspoon ground nutmeg
1 teaspoon dried oregano
$^1/_4$ teaspoon freshly ground
    black pepper

1. In large nonstick skillet, heat oil; add onion. Cook over medium heat, stirring frequently, 3–5 minutes, until onion is softened. Add garlic and ginger; cook, stirring frequently, 2 minutes.
2. Add beef to onion mixture; cook, stirring to break up meat, 4–5 minutes, until beef is no longer pink. Add spinach, rice, tomato, soy sauce and vinegar; cook, stirring frequently, 4 minutes, until mixture is heated through. Stir in nutmeg, oregano and pepper. Divide evenly among 4 plates and serve.

Serving (1 cup) provides: $^1/_4$ Fat, $1^3/_4$ Vegetables, $1^1/_2$ Proteins, 1 Bread.

Per serving: 230 Calories, 8 g Total Fat, 3 g Saturated Fat, 33 mg Cholesterol, 148 mg Sodium, 26 g Total Carbohydrate, 3 g Dietary Fiber, 15 g Protein, 54 mg Calcium.

CORNED BEEF HASH

Makes 4 servings

Serve this filling classic plain, or top each portion with a poached egg. With corn muffins and grilled plum tomatoes, it's a terrific Sunday brunch.

1 teaspoon vegetable oil
1 medium onion, minced
1 medium celery stalk, minced
$^1/_4$ medium green bell pepper, minced
1 tablespoon all-purpose flour
$^1/_2$ cup hot low-sodium chicken broth
12 ounces cooked red potatoes, peeled and finely diced

8 ounces lean cooked corned beef, minced
2 tablespoons minced fresh flat-leaf parsley
$^1/_2$ teaspoon Worcestershire sauce
$^1/_4$ teaspoon freshly ground black pepper, or to taste

1. In small nonstick skillet, heat oil; add onion, celery and bell pepper. Cook over medium heat, stirring frequently, 3–5 minutes, until vegetables are softened. Reduce heat to low; sprinkle vegetable mixture with flour. Cook, stirring constantly, 2 minutes, until flour is dissolved. With wire whisk, stir in broth; continuing to stir, cook 10 minutes, until mixture is thickened. Remove from heat.
2. Gently stir potatoes, beef, parsley, Worcestershire sauce and black pepper into vegetable mixture; set aside to cool slightly.
3. Refrigerate beef mixture, covered, until cool enough to handle. Divide beef mixture into 8 equal portions; form each portion into a $^1/_2$" thick patty.
4. Spray large nonstick skillet with nonstick cooking spray; heat. Add patties; cook over medium heat, turning once, 4 minutes, until patties are browned on both sides. Place 2 patties on each of 4 plates and serve.

Serving (2 patties) provides: $^1/_4$ Fat, $^1/_2$ Vegetable, 2 Proteins, $^3/_4$ Bread, 10 Optional Calories.

Per serving: 166 Calories, 3 g Total Fat, 1 g Saturated Fat, 25 mg Cholesterol, 716 mg Sodium, 22 g Total Carbohydrate, 2 g Dietary Fiber, 14 g Protein, 17 mg Calcium.

VEAL

VEAL MONTICELLO

Makes 4 servings

This quick dish is a must for mushroom lovers! For a hearty meal, serve it with noodles or wild and brown rice pilaf. For a change of pace, substitute skinless boneless turkey breast for the veal.

2 teaspoons vegetable oil
15 ounces boneless lean loin of
  veal, cut into 2" cubes
2 cups sliced mushrooms
1 medium onion, minced
$1/2$ medium carrot, minced
$1/2$ medium celery stalk, minced
2 garlic cloves, minced

4 fluid ounces ($1/2$ cup) dry sherry
$1/2$ cup low-sodium chicken broth
2 teaspoons all-purpose flour
$1/2$ teaspoon dried rosemary leaves,
  crumbled
$1/4$ teaspoon freshly ground black
  pepper

1. In medium nonstick skillet, heat 1 teaspoon of the oil; add veal. Cook over medium heat, turning once, 7–8 minutes, until veal is cooked through and golden brown. With slotted spoon, remove veal from skillet; set aside.
2. In same skillet, heat remaining 1 teaspoon oil; add mushrooms, onion, carrot and celery. Cook over medium heat, stirring frequently, 8–10 minutes, until onions are golden brown. Cover skillet; cook 5 minutes, until mushrooms release their liquid. Uncover; cook, stirring frequently, 5 minutes, until liquid is evaporated. Stir in garlic; cook, stirring frequently, 2 minutes.
3. In small bowl, combine sherry, broth, flour, rosemary and pepper, stirring until flour is dissolved. Stir sherry mixture and veal into vegetable mixture; bring liquid to a boil. Reduce heat to low; simmer, covered, 45 minutes, until veal is very tender and mixture is slightly thickened. Divide evenly among 4 plates and serve.

Serving (3 ounces veal with 1 cup vegetable mixture) provides: $1/2$ Fat, $1^1/2$ Vegetables, 3 Proteins, 35 Optional Calories.

Per serving: 205 Calories, 5 g Total Fat, 1 g Saturated Fat, 83 mg Cholesterol, 95 mg Sodium, 8 g Total Carbohydrate, 1 g Dietary Fiber, 24 g Protein, 26 mg Calcium.

VEAL BIRDS

Makes 4 servings

Serve these stuffed rolls with Parmesan noodles and a green salad. Make the rolls with skinless turkey breast instead of the veal, if you prefer.

Four 3-ounce boneless lean veal cutlets (cut from leg)	2 tablespoons minced fresh flat-leaf parsley
1 teaspoon vegetable oil	$^1/_4$ teaspoon fennel seeds, crushed
$^1/_4$ medium onion, minced	$^1/_4$ teaspoon dried oregano
$^1/_4$ medium celery stalk, minced	$^1/_4$ teaspoon freshly ground black pepper
$^1/_2$ cup cooked long-grain rice	
1 ounce boneless lean cooked Virginia ham, minced	1 cup tomato sauce (no salt added)
	$^1/_4$ cup low-sodium chicken broth

1. Place veal between 2 sheets of wax paper; with meat mallet or bottom of heavy saucepan, gently pound veal to $^1/_8$" thickness. Remove and discard wax paper; set veal aside.
2. In medium nonstick skillet, heat oil; add onion and celery. Cook over medium heat, stirring frequently, 3–5 minutes, until vegetables are softened.
3. Transfer vegetable mixture to medium bowl; stir in rice, ham, parsley, fennel seeds, oregano and pepper.
4. Spread an equal amount of rice mixture over each veal cutlet. Beginning at one short end, roll veal jelly-roll fashion to enclose filling; secure with toothpicks or kitchen string.
5. In same skillet, combine tomato sauce and broth; bring mixture to a boil. Reduce heat to low; add veal "birds," spooning some of the tomato sauce mixture over veal. Simmer, basting veal frequently with sauce mixture, 30 minutes; turn veal over. Continue simmering, adding 1 tablespoon water at a time if mixture becomes too thick, 15–30 minutes longer, until veal is very tender. Divide evenly among 4 plates and serve.

Serving (1 veal bird with $^1/_4$ cup sauce) provides: $^1/_4$ Fat, 1 Vegetable, $2^1/_4$ Proteins, $^1/_4$ Bread.

Per serving: 169 Calories, 3 g Total Fat, 1 g Saturated Fat, 70 mg Cholesterol, 178 mg Sodium, 12 g Total Carbohydrate, 1 g Dietary Fiber, 21 g Protein, 16 mg Calcium.

VEAL PAPRIKASH

Makes 4 servings

For a taste straight from Budapest, serve this rich, quick-to-fix classic with cucumber salad and poppy-seed noodles.

15 ounces boneless lean veal cutlets (cut from leg)	$^1/_4$ teaspoon freshly ground black pepper
$^1/_2$ cup fresh lemon juice	2 teaspoons vegetable oil
$^3/_4$ cup nonfat sour cream	2 medium onions, thinly sliced
2 teaspoons cornstarch	1 tablespoon + 1 teaspoon mild or
1 tablespoon + 1 teaspoon all-purpose flour	1 teaspoon hot Hungarian paprika
$^1/_4$ teaspoon salt	$^3/_4$ cup low-sodium chicken broth

1. Place veal between 2 sheets of wax paper; with meat mallet or bottom of heavy saucepan, gently pound veal to $^1/_8$" thickness. Remove and discard wax paper; set veal aside.
2. Pour juice into gallon-size sealable plastic bag; add veal. Seal bag, squeezing out air; turn to coat veal. Refrigerate 1 hour, turning bag occasionally.
3. Drain veal, reserving 3 tablespoons of the juice; pat veal dry.
4. In small bowl, combine sour cream, cornstarch and reserved juice, stirring until cornstarch is dissolved; set aside.
5. On sheet of wax paper or paper plate, combine flour, salt and pepper; one at a time, place each veal cutlet into flour mixture, coating one side only.
6. In large nonstick skillet, heat 1 teaspoon of the oil; add veal, flour-side down. Cook over medium heat, turning once, 7–8 minutes, until veal is cooked through and golden brown. With slotted spoon, remove veal from skillet; set aside.
7. In same skillet, heat remaining 1 teaspoon oil; add onions. Cook over medium heat, stirring frequently, 8–10 minutes, until onions are golden brown; reduce heat to low. Sprinkle onions with paprika; cook, stirring constantly, 2–3 minutes, until onions are evenly coated (do not burn).
8. Add broth to onion mixture; bring liquid to a boil, scraping up browned bits from bottom of skillet. Cook over high heat, stirring occasionally, until liquid is reduced in volume by about half; reduce heat to low. Stir reserved sour cream mixture into onion mixture; cook, stirring occasionally, 3 minutes, until mixture comes just to a boil. Reduce heat; add veal, spooning some of the onion mixture over veal. Cook 1–2 minutes, until veal is heated through (do not boil). Divide evenly among 4 plates and serve.

Serving (3 ounces veal with $^1/_2$ cup onion mixture) provides: $^1/_2$ Fat, $^1/_2$ Vegetable, 3 Proteins, 50 Optional Calories.

Per serving: 210 Calories, 5 g Total Fat, 1 g Saturated Fat, 83 mg Cholesterol, 257 mg Sodium, 13 g Total Carbohydrate, 1 g Dietary Fiber, 27 g Protein, 81 mg Calcium.

SPANISH RICE WITH VEAL

Makes 4 servings

Wild rice has a luxurious, nutty flavor that's hard to match. It takes a bit longer to cook than other varieties of rice, but it's well worth it. If you like, substitute brown rice for the wild.

2 teaspoons olive oil	1 teaspoon dried thyme leaves
1 medium red onion, chopped	$^1/_2$ teaspoon paprika
1 medium green bell pepper, diced	$^1/_4$ teaspoon salt
1 medium red bell pepper, diced	12 ounces boneless lean cooked veal, cut into $^1/_2$" cubes
2 garlic cloves, minced	2 cups cooked wild rice
2 medium tomatoes, chopped	$^1/_4$ cup minced fresh flat-leaf parsley
$^1/_4$ teaspoon hot red pepper sauce	

1. In large nonstick skillet, heat oil; add onion. Cook over medium heat, stirring frequently, 8–10 minutes, until onion is golden brown. Add green and red bell peppers and garlic; cook, stirring frequently, 5 minutes, until bell peppers are tender.
2. Add tomatoes, pepper sauce, thyme, paprika and salt to vegetable mixture; cook, stirring frequently, 3–5 minutes, until tomatoes are softened.
3. Add veal and rice to tomato mixture; cook, stirring occasionally, 5 minutes, until mixture is heated through. Remove from heat; stir in parsley. Divide evenly among 4 plates and serve.

Serving (1$^1/_2$ cups) provides: $^1/_2$ Fat, 2$^1/_4$ Vegetables, 3 Proteins, 1 Bread.

Per serving: 294 Calories, 9 g Total Fat, 3 g Saturated Fat, 90 mg Cholesterol, 239 mg Sodium, 27 g Total Carbohydrate, 2 g Dietary Fiber, 27 g Protein, 50 mg Calcium.

BLANQUETTE DE VEAU (VEAL STEW)

Makes 4 servings

For a dish that's ready in half the time, use skinless boneless turkey breast in place of the veal; it needs to simmer only 45 minutes, rather than the hour and a half that the veal requires.

14 ounces boneless lean loin of
  veal, cut into 2" cubes
1 medium carrot, quartered
1 medium onion, quartered
1 medium celery stalk, quartered
6 fresh flat-leaf parsley sprigs
1 bay leaf
$^1/_2$ teaspoon dried thyme leaves
2 cups whole small mushrooms,
  woody ends trimmed
1 cup pearl onions

1 tablespoon + 1 teaspoon
  all-purpose flour
$^1/_3$ cup fat-free egg substitute
2 tablespoons nonfat cream cheese,
  softened
2 teaspoons fresh lemon juice
Pinch ground nutmeg
Freshly ground black pepper,
  to taste
1 tablespoon minced fresh flat-leaf
  parsley, to garnish

1. To prepare broth, place veal into medium saucepan; add water to cover. Bring liquid to a boil; with slotted spoon, skim off foam that accumulates on surface. Reduce heat to low; cook, continuing to skim off accumulated foam, 20 minutes (do not boil).
2. Add carrot, quartered onion, celery, parsley sprigs, bay leaf and thyme to veal mixture; cook, covered, $1^1/_2$ hours, until veal is very tender. With slotted spoon, remove veal from liquid; set aside.
3. Place medium sieve over medium bowl. Strain liquid through sieve, reserving liquid; discard solids. Let liquid stand 15–20 minutes, until fat accumulates on top; with paper towels or large spoon, remove fat.
4. To prepare stew, in same saucepan, combine mushrooms, pearl onions, veal and $1^1/_2$ cups* of the prepared broth. In small bowl, with wire whisk, combine flour and 2 tablespoons cold water, blending until flour is dissolved. Stir dissolved flour into veal mixture; bring liquid to a boil. Reduce heat to low; simmer, stirring frequently, 15 minutes, until mixture is slightly thickened.
5. Meanwhile, in blender or food processor, combine egg substitute, cream cheese, juice, nutmeg and pepper; purée until smooth.

---

* Divide remaining broth into 1-cup portions; cool, then freeze, covered, until solid. Use in recipes calling for veal or beef broth, or serve on its own.

6. Remove veal mixture from heat; stir in cream cheese mixture. Return mixture to heat; cook over low heat, stirring constantly, 2–3 minutes, until heated through (do not boil). Divide evenly among 4 bowls, sprinkle with minced parsley and serve.

Serving (1¹/₂ cups) provides: 1¹/₂ Vegetables, 3 Proteins, 20 Optional Calories.

Per serving: 172 Calories, 4 g Total Fat, 1 g Saturated Fat, 80 mg Cholesterol, 166 mg Sodium, 10 g Total Carbohydrate, 1 g Dietary Fiber, 25 g Protein, 69 mg Calcium.

One cup broth provides: 20 Optional Calories.

Per serving: 20 Calories, 0 g Total Fat, 0 g Saturated Fat, 0 mg Cholesterol, 70 mg Sodium, 0 g Total Carbohydrate, 0 g Dietary Fiber, 5 g Protein, 0 mg Calcium.

VEAL STEW WITH TOMATOES, ARTICHOKES AND SAFFRON

Makes 4 servings

1 teaspoon vegetable oil
4 medium onions, chopped
$^1/_2$ medium red or yellow bell
    pepper, diced
2 large garlic cloves, minced
15 ounces boneless lean loin of
    veal, cut into 2" cubes
1 cup canned whole Italian
    tomatoes (no salt added),
    chopped (reserve juice)
4 fluid ounces ($^1/_2$ cup) dry
    white wine

$^1/_4$ cup low-sodium chicken broth
$^1/_2$ teaspoon dried rosemary leaves,
    crumbled
$^1/_4$ teaspoon freshly ground black
    pepper
Pinch saffron threads, dissolved in
    1 tablespoon hot water
One 10-ounce package thawed
    frozen artichoke hearts
2 tablespoons minced fresh flat-leaf
    parsley, to garnish

1. In large nonstick skillet, heat $^1/_2$ teaspoon of the oil; add onions and bell pepper. Cook over medium heat, stirring frequently, 6–7 minutes, until onions are lightly browned. Add garlic; cook, stirring frequently, 2 minutes. Remove vegetable mixture from skillet; set aside.

2. In same skillet, heat remaining $^1/_2$ teaspoon oil; add veal. Cook over medium heat, stirring frequently, 8–10 minutes, until veal is browned on all sides and cooked through. Add tomatoes with juice, wine, broth, rosemary, black pepper, saffron and reserved vegetable mixture; cook, scraping up browned bits from bottom of skillet, 5 minutes, until heated through and well combined. Reduce heat to low; simmer, covered, stirring occasionally, 1–1$^1/_2$ hours, until veal is tender.

3. Add artichoke hearts to veal mixture; simmer, covered, 30 minutes, until artichoke hearts are cooked through and veal is very tender. Divide evenly among 4 bowls, sprinkle with parsley and serve.

Serving (1$^1/_4$ cups) provides: $^1/_4$ Fat, 2$^3/_4$ Vegetables, 3 Proteins,
25 Optional Calories.

Per serving: 234 Calories, 5 g Total Fat, 1 g Saturated Fat,
85 mg Cholesterol, 240 mg Sodium, 17 g Total Carbohydrate,
5 g Dietary Fiber, 25 g Protein, 77 mg Calcium.

3

PORK & HAM

BRAISED LEG OF PORK

Makes 8 servings

This Mexican-style entrée is delicious hot or cold.

4 large garlic cloves, crushed
1 tablespoon honey
1 teaspoon paprika
$^1/_2$ teaspoon freshly ground
  black pepper
$^1/_2$ teaspoon anise seed, crushed
$^1/_4$ teaspoon cinnamon
Pinch ground cloves or allspice
One 1-pound 14-ounce boneless
  lean leg of pork, rolled and
  tied with kitchen string

6 large or 12 small plum
  tomatoes
2 medium onions, unpeeled
4 large garlic cloves, unpeeled
1 cup low-sodium chicken broth
2 teaspoons pureed canned *chipotles
  en adobo**, or to taste
2 teaspoons unsweetened cocoa
  powder, dissolved in 2 tablespoons hot water

1. In small bowl, combine crushed garlic, honey, paprika, black pepper, anise seed, cinnamon and cloves, mixing to form a paste; rub into pork on all sides. Place pork into gallon-size sealable plastic bag; seal bag, squeezing out air. Refrigerate pork 8–24 hours.
2. Preheat broiler. Line baking sheet with foil.
3. To prepare sauce, place tomatoes, onions and unpeeled garlic onto prepared baking sheet. Broil 6" from heat, turning as they begin to brown, until golden brown on all sides; as each item is done, transfer to medium bowl to cool.
4. Reduce oven temperature to 375° F. Spray a 2-quart shallow baking dish with nonstick cooking spray.
5. Peel vegetables, removing as much skin from tomatoes as possible (leave on skin that is difficult to remove). Transfer to blender or food processor; purée until smooth. Add broth, *chipotles* and dissolved cocoa; process until combined.
6. Place pork into prepared baking dish; roast 20 minutes. Reduce oven temperature to 325° F; top pork with sauce. Bake, covered, basting occasionally with sauce, 50–60 minutes, until pork is cooked through and tender or meat thermometer inserted into center of pork registers 170° F. Transfer pork to cutting board; cover to keep warm.
7. Let sauce stand 15–20 minutes, until fat accumulates on top; with paper towels or large spoon, remove fat.

*Chipotles en adobo—smoked dried jalapeño peppers in a spicy tomato sauce—are available in Latino grocery stores and some supermarkets.

8. Thinly slice pork; arrange slices on serving platter. Serve with sauce.

Serving (3 ounces pork with $^1/_4$ cup sauce) provides: 1 Vegetable, 3 Proteins, 10 Optional Calories.

Per serving: 182 Calories, 6 g Total Fat, 2 g Saturated Fat, 72 mg Cholesterol, 89 mg Sodium, 8 g Total Carbohydrate, 1 g Dietary Fiber, 23 g Protein, 26 mg Calcium.

PORK WITH SPINACH AND CHICK-PEAS

Makes 4 servings

This dish has everything! It's simple to prepare and pretty enough for company, and can be on the dinner table in less than 30 minutes.

1 pound spinach, washed, drained and trimmed
$^1/_4$ teaspoon salt
1 teaspoon olive oil
10 ounces boneless lean pork loin, cut into $^1/_2$" cubes
10 garlic cloves, thinly sliced
$^3/_4$ teaspoon crushed red pepper flakes, or to taste

8 ounces drained cooked chick-peas (garbonzo beans)
$^1/_4$ teaspoon dried thyme leaves
$^1/_4$ teaspoon dried basil
Pinch freshly ground black pepper, or to taste

1. In large nonstick skillet, combine spinach and salt; cook over medium heat, covered, 5 minutes, until wilted. Drain, discarding liquid; squeeze spinach dry. Finely chop spinach; set aside. Wipe skillet dry with paper towel.
2. In same skillet, heat oil; add pork, garlic and pepper flakes. Cook over medium heat, stirring frequently, 8–10 minutes, until pork is browned on all sides and cooked through. Add chick-peas, thyme, basil, black pepper and cooked spinach; cook, tossing constantly, 5 minutes, until mixture is heated through. Divide evenly among 4 plates and serve.

Serving ($^3/_4$ cup) provides: $^1/_4$ Fat, 4 Vegetables, 3 Proteins.

Per serving: 242 Calories, 7 g Total Fat, 2 g Saturated Fat, 42 mg Cholesterol, 267 mg Sodium, 22 g Total Carbohydrate, 5 g Dietary Fiber, 24 g Protein, 171 mg Calcium.

BRAISED PORK CHOPS

Makes 4 servings

Today's pork is very lean compared to the pork of a few years ago; for tender, juicy results, braise it over low heat. For a wonderful meal for family or guests, serve this aromatic dish with wild rice or oven-roasted sweet potatoes.

1 teaspoon vegetable oil	$^1/_4$ teaspoon dried rosemary leaves,
Four 5-ounce lean pork loin chops	crumbled
2 cups sliced mushrooms	$^1/_4$ teaspoon freshly ground black
1 medium onion, minced	pepper
$^1/_2$ cup low-sodium chicken	$^1/_2$ cup nonfat cream cheese,
broth	softened
2 fluid ounces ($^1/_4$ cup) dry	$^1/_4$ cup skim milk
sherry	

1. In medium nonstick skillet, heat oil; add pork chops. Cook over medium-high heat, turning once, 2 minutes, until browned on both sides. Remove pork chops from skillet; set aside.
2. In same skillet, combine mushrooms and onion; cook over medium heat, stirring frequently, 8–10 minutes, until vegetables are golden brown. Stir in broth, sherry, rosemary and pepper; bring liquid to a boil. Add browned pork chops; baste with some of the liquid in skillet. Reduce heat to low; simmer, covered, basting occasionally with liquid in skillet, 30 minutes, until pork chops are cooked through and very tender.
3. Meanwhile, in small bowl, combine cheese and milk; with electric mixer, beat until smooth.*
4. Stir cheese mixture into pork chop mixture; cook until just heated through (do not boil). Place 1 pork chop on each of 4 plates; top each portion with an equal amount of the vegetable mixture.

Serving (1 pork chop with $^1/_2$ cup vegetable mixture) provides: $^1/_4$ Fat, $1^1/_4$ Vegetables, 3 Proteins, 50 Optional Calories.

Per serving: 239 Calories, 7 g Total Fat, 2 g Saturated Fat, 75 mg Cholesterol, 236 mg Sodium, 7 g Total Carbohydrate, 1 g Dietary Fiber, 31 g Protein, 133 mg Calcium.

---

* If desired, cheese mixture may be prepared in blender or food processor; purée until smooth.

STUFFED PORK CHOPS

Makes 4 servings

When these chops are cut open, they reveal a jewel-like center of spiced fruit. Serve them with baked sweet potatoes or a roasted chestnut purée.

$^1/_2$ cup apple cider or juice
$1^1/_2$ ounces mixed dried fruit, minced
1 teaspoon vegetable oil
$^1/_2$ medium onion, minced
$^1/_2$ teaspoon dried sage leaves, crumbled
$^1/_4$ teaspoon freshly ground black pepper

Four 5-ounce lean pork loin chops ($^3/_4$" thick), sliced horizontally to form a pocket
$^3/_4$ cup low-sodium chicken broth
1 teaspoon Worcestershire sauce
1 teaspoon cornstarch, dissolved in 1 tablespoon cold water

1. Preheat oven to 325° F.
2. In small bowl, combine $^1/_4$ cup of the cider and the dried fruit; set aside.
3. In large ovenproof skillet, heat $^1/_2$ teaspoon of the oil; add onion. Cook over medium heat, stirring frequently, 6–7 minutes, until lightly browned. Remove from heat.
4. Add sage, pepper and cooked onion to dried fruit mixture; stir to combine.
5. Stuff each pork pocket with one-fourth of the dried fruit mixture; secure open edges with toothpicks.
6. In same skillet, heat remaining $^1/_2$ teaspoon oil; add stuffed pork chops. Cook over medium-high heat, turning once, 2 minutes, until browned on both sides. Stir in broth, Worcestershire sauce and remaining $^1/_4$ cup cider; bake, covered, basting occasionally with broth mixture, 1 hour, until pork chops are cooked through and very tender. With slotted spatula, place 1 pork chop on each of 4 plates; cover to keep warm.
7. Place skillet over high heat; bring liquid to a boil. Cook until liquid is reduced in volume to about 1 cup; reduce heat to low. Stir in dissolved cornstarch; simmer, stirring constantly, 3 minutes, until mixture is slightly thickened. Pour evenly over pork chops and serve.

Serving (1 stuffed pork chop with $^1/_4$ cup sauce) provides: $^1/_4$ Fat, $^3/_4$ Fruit, $^1/_4$ Vegetable, 3 Proteins, 5 Optional Calories.

Per serving: 226 Calories, 8 g Total Fat, 3 g Saturated Fat, 67 mg Cholesterol, 97 mg Sodium, 13 g Total Carbohydrate, 1 g Dietary Fiber, 25 g Protein, 33 mg Calcium.

PORK AND LIMA BEAN STEW

Makes 4 servings

6 ounces dried lima beans
2 teaspoons vegetable oil
4 medium onions, chopped
2 medium celery stalks, minced
1 medium green bell pepper, minced
5 ounces boneless lean pork loin, diced
1 bay leaf

2 cups canned whole Italian tomatoes (no salt added), chopped (reserve juice)
1 teaspoon granulated sugar
$^3/_4$ teaspoon dried thyme leaves
$^1/_4$ cup minced fresh flat-leaf parsley
$^3/_4$ teaspoon salt
$^1/_2$ teaspoon freshly ground black pepper

1. Place beans into medium bowl; add cold water to cover. Let stand overnight.
2. Drain beans; discard liquid. In medium saucepan, bring 2 cups water to a boil; add beans. Reduce heat to low; simmer, covered, adding $^1/_4$ cup boiling water at a time if mixture begins to stick, 1 hour, until beans are tender. Remove from heat.
3. Meanwhile, in large nonstick skillet, heat 1 teaspoon of the oil; add onions, celery and bell pepper. Cook over medium heat, stirring frequently, 8–10 minutes, until onions are golden brown. Transfer vegetable mixture to saucepan with cooked beans; set aside.
4. In same skillet, heat remaining 1 teaspoon oil; add pork. Cook over medium heat, stirring frequently, 5–6 minutes, until pork is browned on all sides and cooked through. Add, bay leaf, tomatoes with juice, sugar and thyme; cook, scraping up browned bits from bottom of skillet, 5 minutes, until heated through and well combined.
5. Add pork mixture to bean mixture; bring mixture to a boil. Reduce heat to low; simmer, covered, stirring occasionally, adding 1 tablespoon water at a time if mixture begins to stick, 1 hour, until beans and pork are very tender.
6. Stir in parsley, salt and black pepper; remove and discard bay leaf. Divide evenly among 4 plates and serve.

Serving (1 cup) provides: $^1/_2$ Fat, $2^3/_4$ Vegetables, 3 Proteins, 5 Optional Calories.

Per serving: 287 Calories, 5 g Total Fat, 1 g Saturated Fat, 21 mg Cholesterol, 651 mg Sodium, 43 g Total Carbohydrate, 11 g Dietary Fiber, 19 g Protein, 113 mg Calcium.

ROSEMARY PORK STEW

Makes 4 servings

Redolent of rosemary, oregano and thyme, this aromatic stew is chock-full of colorful vegetables. For a different flavor, substitute boneless lean loin or leg of lamb for the pork.

$^1/_2$ teaspoon salt
$^1/_4$ teaspoon paprika
$^1/_4$ teaspoon minced fresh oregano
$^1/_4$ teaspoon minced fresh thyme leaves
$^1/_4$ teaspoon freshly ground black pepper
10 ounces boneless lean pork loin, cut into 2" cubes
2 teaspoons olive oil
2 medium carrots, diced

1 cup parsnips, diced
5-ounces all-purpose potato, pared and diced
1 medium onion, diced
2 cups low-sodium beef broth
2 large or 4 small plum tomatoes, seeded and diced
1 tablespoon + 1 teaspoon minced fresh rosemary leaves, or $1^1/_4$ teaspoons dried, crumbled
2 large garlic cloves, minced

1. On sheet of wax paper or paper plate, combine $^1/_4$ teaspoon of the salt, the paprika, oregano, thyme and pinch of the pepper; add pork, turning to coat evenly.
2. In large nonstick saucepan, heat oil; add pork. Cook over high heat, stirring frequently, 2 minutes, until browned on all sides. Add carrots, parsnips, potato and onion; cook, stirring constantly, 1–2 minutes, until vegetables begin to soften.
3. Add broth, tomatoes, rosemary, garlic, remaining $^1/_4$ teaspoon salt and remaining pepper to pork mixture; bring liquid to a boil. Reduce heat to low; simmer, stirring occasionally, 30 minutes, until vegetables are tender and pork is cooked through. Divide evenly among 4 plates and serve.

Serving (1 cup) provides: $^1/_2$ Fat, $1^3/_4$ Vegetables, 2 Proteins, $^3/_4$ Bread, 10 Optional Calories.

Per serving: 224 Calories, 7 g Total Fat, 2 g Saturated Fat, 42 mg Cholesterol, 405 mg Sodium, 21 g Total Carbohydrate, 4 g Dietary Fiber, 20 g Protein, 56 mg Calcium.

Pork Stew with Corn and Beans

Makes 4 servings

6 ounces dried red kidney beans
1 teaspoon vegetable oil
2 medium onions, chopped
$^1/_2$ medium green bell pepper, minced
2 large garlic cloves, minced
5 ounces boneless lean pork loin, diced
1 tablespoon chili powder
$^1/_2$ teaspoon dried oregano
$^1/_4$ teaspoon ground cumin
$^1/_4$ teaspoon ground coriander

$^1/_4$ teaspoon cinnamon
Pinch freshly ground black pepper
2 cups canned whole Italian tomatoes (no salt added), chopped (reserve juice)
2 teaspoons firmly packed dark brown sugar
1 cup diced pared acorn squash
$1^1/_2$ cups fresh or thawed frozen corn kernels
2 tablespoons minced fresh cilantro
$^1/_2$ teaspoon salt

1. Place beans into medium bowl; add cold water to cover. Let stand overnight.
2. Drain beans; discard liquid. In medium saucepan, bring 2 cups water to a boil; add beans. Reduce heat to low; simmer, covered, adding $^1/_4$ cup boiling water at a time if mixture begins to stick, 1 hour, until beans are tender. Remove from heat. Drain beans; set aside.
3. Preheat oven to 325° F. Spray $1^1/_2$-quart casserole with nonstick cooking spray.
4. Meanwhile, in medium nonstick skillet, heat $^1/_2$ teaspoon of the oil; add onions and bell pepper. Cook over medium heat, stirring frequently, 6–7 minutes, until onions are lightly browned. Add garlic; cook, stirring frequently, 2 minutes. Remove vegetable mixture from skillet; set aside.
5. In same skillet, heat remaining $^1/_2$ teaspoon oil; add pork. Cook over medium heat, stirring frequently, 5–6 minutes, until pork is browned on all sides and cooked through. Reduce heat to low; add chili powder, oregano, cumin, coriander, cinnamon and pepper. Cook, stirring constantly, 2 minutes. Add tomatoes with juice, sugar and $^1/_2$ cup water; cook, scraping up browned bits from bottom of skillet, 5 minutes, until heated through and well combined. Remove from heat.
6. Add cooked beans and reserved vegetable mixture to pork mixture; stir to combine. Transfer mixture to prepared casserole; bake, covered, 1–$1^1/_2$ hours, until pork is tender. Remove pork mixture from oven; leave oven on.
7. Add squash and corn to pork mixture; bake, covered, 30 minutes, until squash is tender. Stir in cilantro and salt. Divide evenly among 4 bowls and serve.

Serving (1¹/₂ cups) provides: ¹/₄ Fat, 1³/₄ Vegetables, 3 Proteins, 1 Bread, 10 Optional Calories.

Per serving: 330 Calories, 5 g Total Fat, 1 g Saturated Fat, 21 mg Cholesterol, 530 mg Sodium, 54 g Total Carbohydrate, 10 g Dietary Fiber, 22 g Protein, 140 mg Calcium.

ASIAN STUFFED PEPPERS

Makes 4 servings

2 medium scallions, minced
5 large garlic cloves, minced
2 teaspoons minced pared fresh
　ginger root
15 ounces lean ground pork
1 tablespoon cornstarch
1 tablespoon reduced-sodium soy
　sauce

1 tablespoon rice wine vinegar
4 medium green or red bell peppers,
　halved lengthwise and seeded
¹/₂ cup low-sodium chicken broth
1 tablespoon minced fresh cilantro,
　to garnish
1 tablespoon minced fresh flat-leaf
　parsley, to garnish

1. Preheat oven to 350° F.
2. Spray medium nonstick skillet with nonstick cooking spray; heat. Add scallions, garlic and ginger; cook over high heat, stirring constantly, 15–20 seconds, until fragrant. Remove from heat; transfer to medium bowl to cool.
3. Add pork, cornstarch, soy sauce and vinegar to cooled scallion mixture; mix thoroughly. Stuff each bell pepper half with an equal amount of pork mixture; place, stuffed-side up, into 2-quart shallow casserole. Add broth to casserole; bake, loosely covered, 30–35 minutes, until stuffing is cooked through and peppers are tender. Bake, uncovered, 10 minutes, until stuffing begins to brown. Place 2 pepper halves on each of 4 plates, sprinkle with cilantro and parsley and serve.

Serving (2 stuffed pepper halves) provides: 2 Vegetables, 3 Proteins, 10 Optional Calories.

Per serving: 217 Calories, 10 g Total Fat, 3 g Saturated Fat, 68 mg Cholesterol, 240 mg Sodium, 11 g Total Carbohydrate, 2 g Dietary Fiber, 22 g Protein, 49 mg Calcium.

CABBAGE SOUP WITH SWEDISH MEATBALLS

Makes 12 servings

Like many hearty soups, this one tastes even better the day after it's made. Be sure to drop the meatballs into the soup *gently*, since they are fragile when uncooked.

2 teaspoons olive oil
12 cups coarsely chopped green cabbage
2 medium carrots, chopped
3 tablespoons firmly packed light or dark brown sugar
10 cups low-sodium chicken broth

12 ounces lean ground pork
12 ounces lean ground veal
1 tablespoon + $^1/_4$ teaspoon ground allspice
$^1/_2$ teaspoon salt
$^1/_2$ teaspoon freshly ground black pepper

1. In large pot or Dutch oven, heat oil; add cabbage and carrots. Cook over medium heat, stirring frequently, 3–4 minutes, until cabbage releases its liquid.
2. Meanwhile, in small bowl, combine brown sugar and $^1/_4$ cup water, stirring until sugar is dissolved.
3. Stir dissolved sugar into cabbage mixture; bring liquid to a boil. Reduce heat to low; simmer, stirring occasionally, 15 minutes, until cabbage is tender.
4. Add broth to cabbage mixture; bring liquid to a boil. Reduce heat to low; simmer 10 minutes.
5. Meanwhile, in large bowl, combine pork, veal, allspice, salt and pepper; form into 36 equal meatballs.
6. Gently drop meatballs into broth mixture; simmer 8–12 minutes, until meatballs are cooked through. Divide evenly among 12 bowls and serve.

Serving (1 cup soup with 3 meatballs) provides: $2^1/_4$ Vegetables, $1^1/_2$ Proteins, 35 Optional Calories.

Per serving: 151 Calories, 7 g Total Fat, 2 g Saturated Fat, 41 mg Cholesterol, 249 mg Sodium, 11 g Total Carbohydrate, 2 g Dietary Fiber, 15 g Protein, 69 mg Calcium.

Pork-Stuffed Cabbage Casserole

Makes 4 servings

Serve this homey classic with black bread and a cucumber salad.

8 large green cabbage leaves
10 ounces lean ground pork
$^1/_2$ medium onion, minced
$^1/_2$ medium celery stalk, minced
1 small clove garlic, minced
1 small Granny Smith apple,
  pared, cored and finely diced
$^1/_2$ cup cooked brown rice
2 tablespoons minced fresh flat-
  leaf parsley

2 tablespoons apple juice or cider
1 teaspoon cider vinegar
$^1/_2$ teaspoon salt
$^1/_4$ teaspoon dried thyme leaves
$^1/_4$ teaspoon dried sage leaves,
  crumbled
$^1/_4$ teaspoon freshly ground black
  pepper
1 cup nonfat sour cream
$^1/_4$ teaspoon paprika, to garnish

1. Preheat oven to 325° F. Spray 2-quart shallow baking dish with nonstick cooking spray.
2. Fill a large bowl with cold water. In large pot of boiling water, cook cabbage leaves, one at a time, 2 minutes, until just tender; remove with tongs and immediately plunge into cold water to cool. Transfer to paper towels to drain.
3. Meanwhile, spray medium nonstick skillet with nonstick cooking spray; heat. Add pork and onion; cook, stirring to break up meat, 4–5 minutes, until no longer pink. Add celery and garlic; cook, stirring constantly, 2 minutes, until celery is just tender. Remove from heat. Add apple, rice, parsley, juice, vinegar, salt, thyme, sage and pepper to pork mixture; stir to combine.
4. Place cabbage leaves, outer-side down, onto work surface. Place an equal amount of pork mixture about 1" from base of each leaf; fold base of leaves over filling. Fold sides of leaves inward, overlapping if necessary; roll leaves from base toward tip to enclose.
5. Place stuffed leaves, seam-side down, into prepared baking dish. Spread leaves evenly with sour cream; sprinkle evenly with paprika. Bake, loosely covered, 30 minutes, until heated through. Place 2 stuffed leaves on each of 4 plates and serve.

Serving (2 stuffed cabbage leaves) provides: $^1/_4$ Fruit, $1^1/_4$ Vegetables, 2 Proteins, $^1/_4$ Bread, 45 Optional Calories.

Per serving: 271 Calories, 14 g Total Fat, 5 g Saturated Fat, 49 mg Cholesterol, 366 mg Sodium, 17 g Total Carbohydrate, 2 g Dietary Fiber, 17 g Protein, 124 mg Calcium.

CORN PONE CASSEROLE

Makes 6 servings

Spicy and earthy, this makes a perfect meal when it's nippy out. Serve with a simple salad and a mug of beer.

1¹/₂ teaspoons vegetable oil
4 medium onions, chopped
¹/₂ medium red bell pepper, minced
1 medium jalapeño pepper, seeded, deveined and minced (wear gloves to prevent irritation)
14 ounces lean ground pork
2 tablespoons chili powder
1 cup fresh or thawed frozen corn kernels
³/₄ cup tomato sauce (no salt)
¹/₄ cup low-sodium chicken broth

¹/₄ teaspoon freshly ground black pepper
¹/₄ teaspoon ground red pepper, or to taste
1¹/₄ cups yellow cornmeal
³/₄ cup all-purpose flour
2¹/₂ teaspoons double-acting baking powder
¹/₂ teaspoon salt
Pinch ground cumin
1 cup + 2 tablespoons skim milk
1 egg, beaten

1. Preheat oven to 400° F. Spray 2-quart casserole with nonstick cooking spray.
2. In large nonstick skillet, heat ¹/₂ teaspoon of the oil; add onions and bell and jalapeño peppers. Cook over medium heat, stirring frequently, 6–7 minutes, until onions are lightly browned. Remove vegetable mixture from skillet; set aside.
3. In same skillet, cook pork, stirring to break up meat, 4–5 minutes, until no longer pink. Add chili powder; cook, stirring constantly, 1 minute. Add corn, tomato sauce, broth, black and ground red peppers and reserved vegetable mixture; cook, stirring constantly, 1 minute, until thoroughly combined.
4. Transfer pork mixture to prepared casserole; set aside.
5. In medium bowl, combine cornmeal, flour, baking powder, salt and cumin. Add milk, egg and remaining 1 teaspoon oil; stir until just blended (do not overmix). Spread cornmeal mixture over pork mixture; bake 25–30 minutes, until topping is golden brown. Divide evenly among 6 plates and serve.

Serving (one-sixth of casserole) provides: ¹/₄ Fat, 1¹/₂ Vegetables, 2 Proteins, 3 Breads, 20 Optional Calories.

Per serving: 273 Calories, 9 g Total Fat, 2 g Saturated Fat, 79 mg Cholesterol, 508 mg Sodium, 51 g Total Carbohydrate, 5 g Dietary Fiber, 22 g Protein, 215 mg Calcium.

PORK AND BLACK BEAN STIR-FRY

Makes 4 servings

8 ounces boneless lean pork loin, finely diced

1 teaspoon black bean sauce with chiles*

1 teaspoon reduced-sodium soy sauce

$1/2$ teaspoon granulated sugar

$1/2$ teaspoon freshly ground black pepper

$1/4$ teaspoon ground red pepper, or to taste

1 teaspoon vegetable oil

1 tablespoon minced pared fresh ginger root

4 large garlic cloves, minced

1 cup low-sodium chicken broth

4 ounces drained cooked black beans

4 medium scallions, sliced

1 medium celery stalk, sliced

$1^1/2$ teaspoons cornstarch, dissolved in 1 tablespoon cold water

1 teaspoon oriental sesame oil

2 cups hot steamed long-grain rice

2 tablespoons minced fresh cilantro, to garnish

1. In medium bowl, combine pork, bean and soy sauces, sugar and black and ground red peppers; set aside.
2. In wok or large nonstick skillet, heat vegetable oil; add ginger and garlic. Cook over high heat, stirring constantly, 10 seconds, until fragrant. Add pork mixture; cook, stirring to break up meat, 4–5 minutes, until no longer pink.
3. Add broth to pork mixture; cook, stirring constantly, 2 minutes, until liquid comes to a boil. Add beans, scallions, celery and dissolved cornstarch; cook, stirring constantly, 2–3 minutes, until liquid is slightly thickened. Remove from heat; stir in sesame oil.
4. Spoon rice onto serving platter; top with pork mixture. Serve sprinkled with cilantro.

Serving ($^3/4$ cup pork mixture, $^1/2$ cup rice) provides: $^1/2$ Fat, $^1/4$ Vegetable, 2 Proteins, 1 Bread, 15 Optional Calories.

Per serving with pork loin: 298 Calories, 7 g Total Fat, 2 g Saturated Fat, 33 mg Cholesterol, 131 mg Sodium, 40 g Total Carbohydrate, 1 g Dietary Fiber, 19 g Protein, 51 mg Calcium.

*Black bean sauce with chiles is available in most Asian groceries and gourmet food stores.

TOAD IN THE HOLE

Makes 4 servings

The British have a penchant for unusual food names, such as Chip Butties, Gooseberry Fool and Bubble and Squeak. This simple sausage-in-batter dish is quick to make and delicious in spite of the funny title.

8 ounces cooked reduced-fat pork sausage links, cut into 12 equal pieces

2 medium onions, minced

1 cup minus 1 tablespoon all-purpose flour

1 teaspoon double-acting baking powder

$^1/_2$ teaspoon salt

$^3/_4$ cup skim milk

$^1/_3$ cup fat-free egg substitute

1 egg, beaten

1. Preheat oven to 425° F. Spray 9" round baking dish with nonstick cooking spray.
2. Arrange sausages in a single layer in prepared baking dish; set aside.
3. Spray medium nonstick skillet with nonstick cooking spray; heat. Add onions; cook over medium heat, stirring frequently, 8–10 minutes, until onions are golden brown. Transfer half the onions to baking dish with sausages; set remaining onions aside.
4. Into medium bowl, sift flour, baking powder and salt; make a well in center of flour mixture.
5. In small bowl, combine milk, egg substitute and egg; pour into well. With wire whisk, stir milk mixture, slowly incorporating flour mixture, until flour is evenly moistened and mixture forms a smooth dough. Stir in reserved cooked onions; pour over sausage mixture. Bake 30–35 minutes, until puffed and well browned. Divide evenly among 4 plates and serve immediately.

Serving (one-fourth of mixture) provides: $^1/_2$ Vegetable, $2^1/_2$ Proteins, $1^1/_4$ Breads, 15 Optional Calories.

Per serving: 235 Calories, 4 g Total Fat, 1 g Saturated Fat, 73 mg Cholesterol, 848 mg Sodium, 33 g Total Carbohydrate, 1 g Dietary Fiber, 17 g Protein, 152 mg Calcium.

KALE SOUP WITH CHORIZO

Makes 8 servings

Most supermarkets carry a wonderful variety of greens these days; don't be afraid to experiment with some you've never tried before. This soup features kale; if it's new to you, you're in for a treat with its rich, mild flavor. If you want a milder sausage than chorizo in this robust soup, use linguiça instead.

2 teaspoons olive oil
2 medium onions, chopped
8 cups low-sodium chicken broth
2 pounds 8 ounces all-purpose
  potatoes, pared and sliced
4 large garlic cloves, minced

1 pound 8 ounces kale, trimmed,
  well-washed and chopped
12 ounces drained cooked red
  kidney beans
7 ounces cooked chorizo sausage,
  halved lengthwise and sliced

1. In large nonstick saucepan, heat oil; add onions. Cook over medium heat, stirring frequently, 8–10 minutes, until onions are golden brown.
2. Add broth, potatoes and garlic to onion mixture; bring liquid to a boil. Reduce heat to low; simmer, stirring occasionally, 10–15 minutes, until potatoes are tender.
3. Stir kale into broth mixture; simmer, stirring occasionally, 5 minutes, until kale is tender.
4. Stir beans and chorizo into broth mixture; simmer, stirring occasionally, 5 minutes, until heated through. Divide evenly among 8 bowls and serve.

Serving (1 cup) provides: $1/4$ Fat, $3^1/4$ Vegetables, $1^1/4$ Proteins, 1 Bread, 60 Optional Calories.

Per serving: 335 Calories, 12 g Total Fat, 4 g Saturated Fat, 21 mg Cholesterol, 482 mg Sodium, 46 g Total Carbohydrate, 10 g Dietary Fiber, 18 g Protein, 168 mg Calcium.

White Bean–Sausage Stew

Makes 4 servings

Similar to cassoulet, this simple stew has the flavors of the French classic but can be prepared in a fraction of the time.

2 teaspoons olive oil
2 medium onions, chopped
2 medium celery stalks, chopped
$^1/_2$ medium carrot, chopped
3 garlic cloves, minced
2 cups canned whole Italian
tomatoes (no salt added),
coarsely chopped (reserve
juice)

$1^1/_2$ teaspoons minced fresh
thyme or rosemary leaves, or
$^1/_2$ teaspoon dried, crumbled
1 bay leaf
12 ounces drained cooked white
beans
6 ounces cooked kielbasa, cut into
$^1/_4$" slices

1. Preheat oven to 350° F.
2. In large ovenproof pot or Dutch oven, heat oil; add onions, celery and carrot. Cook over medium heat, stirring frequently, 8–10 minutes, until onions are golden brown. Add garlic; cook, stirring frequently, 2 minutes.
3. Add tomatoes with juice, thyme and bay leaf to vegetable mixture; bring mixture to a boil. Remove from heat; stir in beans and kielbasa. Bake, covered, 45 minutes, until mixture is heated through and flavors are blended; remove and discard bay leaf. Divide evenly among 4 plates and serve.

Serving (1 cup) provides: $^1/_2$ Fat, 2 Vegetables, 3 Proteins.

Per serving: 323 Calories, 15 g Total Fat, 5 g Saturated Fat, 28 mg Cholesterol, 678 mg Sodium, 34 g Total Carbohydrate, 5 g Dietary Fiber, 16 g Protein, 154 mg Calcium.

DEEP-DISH SAUSAGE PIZZA

Makes 4 servings

Pizza is pizza, right? Not anymore. This homemade pizza, with crisp vegetables, flavorful sausage, melted cheese and fresh herbs, redefines pizza—a delicious meal that's as fun to make as it is to eat!

1 teaspoon yellow or white cornmeal

1 teaspoon all-purpose flour

8 ounces refrigerated, thawed frozen or ready-made pizza crust dough

$1/2$ cup tomato sauce (no salt added)

$1/2$ medium green bell pepper, sliced

$1/2$ medium onion, thinly sliced

4 ounces cooked sweet or hot Italian pork sausage, crumbled

$1 1/2$ ounces part-skim mozzarella cheese, grated

2 tablespoons minced fresh basil

$1/4$ teaspoon freshly ground black pepper, or to taste

1 garlic clove, minced

1. Preheat oven to 450° F. Sprinkle 8" square baking pan evenly with cornmeal; set aside.
2. Sprinkle flour onto work surface. Place dough onto floured surface; turn to coat. With rolling pin or fingers, stretch dough into 12" circle; transfer to prepared baking pan, pressing edges against sides of pan to form a rim.
3. Spread tomato sauce evenly onto prepared dough; top sauce evenly with bell pepper and onion. Sprinkle vegetables evenly with sausage, cheese, basil, black pepper and garlic; bake 20 minutes, until cheese is melted and crust is crispy. Cut into 4 equal pieces and serve at once.

Serving (one-fourth of pie) provides: 1 Vegetable, $1 1/2$ Proteins, 2 Breads, 5 Optional Calories.

Per serving: 295 Calories, 11 g Total Fat, 4 g Saturated Fat, 28 mg Cholesterol, 630 mg Sodium, 33 g Total Carbohydrate, 2 g Dietary Fiber, 14 g Protein, 93 mg Calcium.

STUFFED HAM STEAK

Makes 6 servings

Don't wait until a holiday to enjoy this festive dish! Serve with baked sweet potatoes and steamed fresh spinach.

$^1/_2$ teaspoon vegetable oil
1 medium onion, minced
1 medium celery stalk, minced
1 cup low-sodium chicken broth
$^1/_3$ cup + 2 teaspoons plain dried bread crumbs
2 tablespoons minced fresh flat-leaf parsley
$^1/_2$ teaspoon dried sage leaves, crumbled
$^1/_4$ teaspoon freshly ground black pepper

One 12-ounce boneless lean ham steak ($^1/_2$" thick)
2 teaspoons firmly packed light or dark brown sugar
$^1/_2$ teaspoon dry mustard
Pinch cinnamon
2 fluid ounces ($^1/_4$ cup) dry Marsala wine
2 tablespoons raisins
2 tablespoons orange or apple juice
$^1/_2$ teaspoon cornstarch, dissolved in 1 teaspoon cold water

1. Preheat oven to 325° F. Spray 2-quart shallow baking dish with nonstick cooking spray.
2. In medium nonstick skillet, heat oil; add onion. Cook over medium heat, stirring frequently, 6–7 minutes, until onion is lightly browned. Remove all but 2 tablespoons cooked onion from skillet; set aside.
3. Add celery and $^1/_4$ cup of the broth to cooked onion in skillet; bring liquid to a boil. Reduce heat to low; simmer 2 minutes, until celery is just tender. Add bread crumbs, parsley, sage and pepper; stir to combine.
4. With sharp knife, lightly score ham at $^1/_2$" intervals, creating a crisscross pattern; turn ham over. Top one side of ham steak with bread crumb mixture; fold other side over filling to enclose. Tie with kitchen string at 1" intervals; place into prepared baking dish.
5. In small bowl, combine sugar, mustard, cinnamon and 1 tablespoon water, stirring to form a thin paste. Spread paste evenly over ham; bake 1 hour, until ham is very tender.
6. Meanwhile, to prepare sauce, in same skillet, combine wine, raisins, juice, remaining $^3/_4$ cup broth and reserved cooked onion; bring liquid to a boil. Reduce heat to low; simmer 10 minutes, until raisins are plump. Stir in dissolved cornstarch; simmer, stirring constantly, 3 minutes, until slightly thickened. Divide ham evenly among 6 plates, top each portion with an equal amount of sauce and serve.

Serving (one-sixth of stuffed ham steak with 2 tablespoons sauce) provides: $^1/_4$ Vegetable, $1^1/_2$ Proteins, $^1/_4$ Bread, 45 Optional Calories.

Per serving: 147 Calories, 4 g Total Fat, 1 g Saturated Fat, 27 mg Cholesterol, 894 mg Sodium, 12 g Total Carbohydrate, 1 g Dietary Fiber, 12 g Protein, 34 mg Calcium.

CABBAGE SOUP WITH HAM

Makes 4 servings

Here's a quick soup that fills you up, but is actually quite light. Serve it with black bread and a sweet-and-sour cucumber salad.

3 cups low-sodium beef broth
2 cups finely shredded green cabbage
2 medium leeks, well-washed and thinly sliced
1 medium carrot, thinly sliced
6 ounces cooked boneless lean Virginia ham, diced
$^1/_4$ teaspoon caraway seeds
1 small Granny Smith apple, pared, cored and finely diced
1 fluid ounce (2 tablespoons) dry white wine
4 ounces cooked red potato, peeled and diced
2 tablespoons minced fresh flat-leaf parsley

1. In large saucepan, bring broth to a boil; add cabbage, leeks, carrot, ham and caraway seeds. Reduce heat to low; simmer, covered, 15 minutes, until carrot is just tender.
2. Add apple and wine to broth mixture; simmer, uncovered, 3 minutes, until apple is just tender. Stir in potato and parsley; simmer 2–3 minutes, until heated through. Divide evenly among 4 bowls and serve.

Serving ($1^1/_2$ cups) provides: $^1/_4$ Fruit, $2^1/_2$ Vegetables, $1^1/_2$ Proteins, $^1/_4$ Bread, 20 Optional Calories.

Per serving: 161 Calories, 2 g Total Fat, 1 g Saturated Fat, 20 mg Cholesterol, 688 mg Sodium, 20 g Total Carbohydrate, 3 g Dietary Fiber, 14 g Protein, 61 mg Calcium.

SPLIT PEA SOUP WITH HAM

Makes 4 servings

This classic soup makes a perfect winter lunch.

2 teaspoons vegetable oil
2 medium onions, diced
2 medium carrots, diced
1 garlic clove, minced
5 cups low-sodium chicken broth
6 ounces dried green split peas

4 ounces cooked boneless lean ham, diced
1 teaspoon minced fresh rosemary leaves
$^1/_4$ cup minced fresh flat-leaf parsley, to garnish

1. In large nonstick saucepan, heat oil; add onions, carrots and garlic. Cook over medium heat, stirring frequently, 3–5 minutes, until onions are softened.
2. Add broth, split peas, ham and rosemary; bring liquid to a boil. Reduce heat to low; simmer, partially covered, stirring occasionally, 1–1$^1/_4$ hours, until peas have dissolved and flavors are blended. Divide evenly among 4 bowls, sprinkle with parsley and serve.

Serving (1$^1/_4$ cups) provides: $^1/_2$ Fat, 1$^1/_2$ Vegetables, 3 Proteins, 25 Optional Calories.

Per serving: 256 Calories, 7 g Total Fat, 2 g Saturated Fat, 16 mg Cholesterol, 494 mg Sodium, 33 g Total Carbohydrate, 3 g Dietary Fiber, 21 g Protein, 62 mg Calcium.

CREAMY TOMATO SOUP WITH HAM

Makes 4 servings

Use your favorite fresh herbs in this rich-tasting soup, and serve it with melba toast and a salad for a pretty, satisfying supper.

1 tablespoon stick margarine
1^1/$_2$ medium onions, minced
1 garlic clove, minced
2 fluid ounces (^{1}/$_4$ cup) dry white wine
2 cups canned whole Italian tomatoes (no salt added), pureed
1 cup canned tomato purée (no salt added)
1 teaspoon granulated sugar
^{1}/$_4$ teaspoon salt

Pinch freshly ground black pepper, or to taste
^{1}/$_2$ cup nonfat sour cream
2 tablespoons evaporated skimmed milk
2 tablespoons minced fresh flat-leaf parsley
1 tablespoon minced fresh basil or other fresh herb
2 ounces cooked boneless lean Virginia ham, diced
Fresh basil leaves, to garnish

1. In medium nonstick saucepan, melt margarine; add onions and garlic. Cook over medium heat, stirring frequently, 3–5 minutes, until onions are softened.
2. Add wine to onion mixture; bring liquid to a boil. Reduce heat to low; simmer 5 minutes, until liquid is evaporated.
3. Add tomatoes, tomato purée, sugar, salt, pepper and ^{1}/$_2$ cup water to onion mixture; bring liquid to a boil. Reduce heat to low; simmer, covered, stirring occasionally, 30 minutes, until flavors are blended (do not scorch).
4. Meanwhile, in small bowl, combine sour cream, milk, parsley and minced basil; set aside.
5. Remove tomato mixture from heat; with wire whisk, stir in all but 1 tablespoon + 1 teaspoon of the sour cream mixture. Add ham; stir to combine.
6. Ladle soup into 4 bowls; top each portion with 1 teaspoon remaining sour cream mixture. Serve garnished with basil leaves.

Serving (1^1/$_4$ cups) provides: ^{3}/$_4$ Fat, 2^1/$_2$ Vegetables, ^{1}/$_2$ Protein, 40 Optional Calories.

Per serving: 151 Calories, 4 g Total Fat, 1 g Saturated Fat, 8 mg Cholesterol, 816 mg Sodium, 19 g Total Carbohydrate, 3 g Dietary Fiber, 8 g Protein, 122 mg Calcium.

HAM AND POTATO GRATIN

Makes 4 servings

We've dressed up a simple and delicious potato gratin to make an entrée that's wonderfully satisfying. All you need to add is a crisp green salad, and dinner is ready!

15 ounces all-purpose potatoes, thinly sliced

7 ounces cooked boneless lean ham, thinly sliced

3/4 ounce grated Parmesan cheese

2 tablespoons minced fresh flat-leaf parsley

1 tablespoon all-purpose flour

2 teaspoons minced fresh rosemary leaves

1 garlic clove, minced

1/2 teaspoon freshly ground black pepper

1 cup skim milk

1. Preheat oven to 350° F. Spray 8" square baking pan with nonstick cooking spray.
2. Arrange one third of the potato slices in prepared pan; top evenly with one half of the ham, one third of the cheese, 1 tablespoon of the parsley, 1 1/2 teaspoons of the flour, one third of the rosemary, half of the garlic and one third of the pepper. Repeat layers; top evenly with remaining potatoes.
3. Pour milk evenly over potato mixture; with back of wooden spoon, press mixture down so that milk penetrates all layers. Sprinkle evenly with remaining cheese, rosemary and pepper. Bake, covered, 1 hour; bake, uncovered, 30 minutes.
4. Increase oven temperature to 425° F; bake 15 minutes, until top of mixture is golden brown. Remove mixture from oven; let stand 10 minutes. Divide evenly among 4 plates and serve.

Serving (one-fourth of mixture) provides: 1/4 Milk, 2 Proteins, 3/4 Bread, 10 Optional Calories.

Per serving: 213 Calories, 5 g Total Fat, 2 g Saturated Fat, 32 mg Cholesterol, 735 mg Sodium, 25 g Total Carbohydrate, 2 g Dietary Fiber, 17 g Protein, 167 mg Calcium.

LAMB

SICILIAN LEG OF LAMB

Makes 18 servings

Here is a feast for a crowd. Serve with cooked farfalle (bow tie–shaped pasta), Arborio rice or parsleyed potatoes.

One 5½–6-pound lean leg of lamb*

1 large garlic clove, thinly sliced

2 teaspoons tomato paste (no salt added)

1½ teaspoons dried oregano

1 teaspoon olive oil

1 garlic clove, crushed

½ teaspoon freshly ground black pepper

½ cup low-sodium chicken broth

4 fluid ounces (½ cup) dry white wine

2 cups canned whole Italian tomatoes (no salt added), pureed

12 large or 20 small pitted black olives, sliced

3 rinsed drained anchovy fillets, minced

2 tablespoons minced fresh flat-leaf parsley

1. With thin-bladed sharp knife, pierce lamb all over, making 1" deep cuts about 1½" apart. With fingertips, spread each cut open and stuff with 1 garlic slice; seal cuts by smoothing with fingertips.
2. In small bowl, combine tomato paste, oregano, oil, crushed garlic and pepper. Spread all but 2 teaspoons tomato paste mixture over lamb; cover remaining mixture. Place lamb into large sealable plastic bag; seal bag, squeezing out air. Refrigerate lamb and tomato paste mixture overnight.
3. Preheat oven to 450° F. Spray large flameproof roasting pan with nonstick cooking spray.
4. Place lamb into prepared roasting pan; reduce oven temperature to 325° F. Roast lamb 2–2½ hours, until cooked through and meat thermometer inserted into center of lamb, not touching bone, registers 165° F for medium-rare; 175° F for well done. Transfer lamb to cutting board; cover to keep warm.
5. To prepare sauce, add broth and wine to roasting pan; cook over medium heat, scraping up browned bits from bottom of pan, 5 minutes, until heated through and well combined. Let liquid stand 15–20 minutes, until fat accumulates on top; with paper towels or large spoon, remove fat.

A 5½–6-pound leg of lamb will yield 3½–4 pounds boned cooked lamb. Refrigerate remaining lamb, covered, or freeze to use at another time.

6. Transfer liquid to medium saucepan; stir in tomatoes, olives, anchovies, parsley and reserved tomato paste mixture. Bring mixture to a boil; cook 5 minutes, until mixture is slightly reduced in volume.
7. Slice lamb; arrange 3 pounds 6 ounces lamb on serving platter.* Top with sauce.

Serving (3 ounces lamb with 3 tablespoons sauce) provides: $^1/_4$ Vegetable, 3 Proteins, 15 Optional Calories.

Per serving: 183 Calories, 7 g Total Fat, 2 g Saturated Fat, 76 mg Cholesterol, 157 mg Sodium, 2 g Total Carbohydrate, 0 g Dietary Fiber, 25 g Protein, 23 mg Calcium.

LEG OF LAMB WITH CRAB

Makes 8 servings

Lamb with crab? The combination may sound strange, but once you taste it, you'll agree that this is a match made in heaven! For a filling and satisfying meal your friends and family will love, serve this traditional English roast with roasted potatoes or a purée of steamed or roasted root vegetables.

4 ounces shelled cooked crabmeat, flaked	2 medium onions, coarsely chopped
1 tablespoon minced fresh flat-leaf parsley	$^1/_2$ teaspoon dried thyme leaves
$^1/_2$ teaspoon hot red pepper sauce	$^1/_2$ teaspoon dried marjoram
$^3/_4$ teaspoon mild or hot curry powder	$^1/_2$ teaspoon dried rosemary leaves, crumbled
$^1/_4$ teaspoon salt	$^1/_2$ teaspoon freshly ground black pepper
One 1-pound 14-ounce boneless lean leg of lamb*	1 cup low-sodium lamb or chicken broth
4 medium celery stalks, coarsely chopped	4 fluid ounces ($^1/_2$ cup) dry white wine
2 medium carrots, coarsely chopped	$^1/_2$ cup nonfat cream cheese
	$^1/_4$ cup skim milk
	1 teaspoon cornstarch

1. Preheat oven to 350° F. Spray medium flameproof roasting pan with non-stick cooking spray.
2. To prepare lamb, in medium bowl, combine crabmeat, parsley, pepper sauce, $^1/_4$ teaspoon of the curry powder and the salt. Place lamb, boned-side up, onto work surface; spread with crabmeat mixture to within 1" of edge. Roll lamb to enclose filling; tie with kitchen string at 1" intervals.
3. In prepared roasting pan, combine celery, carrots, onions, thyme, marjoram, rosemary, pepper and remaining $^1/_2$ teaspoon curry powder; set lamb roll onto vegetable mixture. Roast 1 hour and 20 minutes, until lamb is cooked through and tender or meat thermometer inserted into center of roll registers 170° F. Transfer lamb roll to cutting board; cover to keep warm.

* To make delicious fresh lamb broth, ask the butcher to save you the bones from the leg of lamb. Roast bones until brown, then combine in a large pot with vegetables, seasonings and water to cover; cook until broth is rich and flavorful. Drain, discarding solids; refrigerate broth until fat congeals on top, then remove congealed fat, or let liquid stand 15–20 minutes, until fat accumulates on top, then with paper towels or large spoon, remove fat. Use in recipes calling for lamb broth, or serve on its own.

4. To prepare broth, add broth and wine to roasted vegetable mixture; cook over medium heat, scraping up browned bits from bottom of pan, 5 minutes, until heated through and well combined.

5. Place medium sieve over medium bowl. Strain liquid through sieve, reserving liquid; discard solids. Let liquid stand 15–20 minutes, until fat accumulates on top; with paper towels or large spoon, remove fat.

6. Transfer prepared broth to medium saucepan; bring to a boil. Cook 3 minutes, until broth is slightly reduced in volume. Reduce heat to low; simmer 2–3 minutes.

7. Meanwhile, to prepare sauce, in blender or food processor, combine cream cheese, milk and cornstarch; purée until smooth. Stir cream cheese mixture into simmering broth; simmer, stirring constantly, 3 minutes, until thickened and heated through.

8. Cut lamb roll into 16 equal slices; arrange on serving platter. Serve lamb slices with sauce.

Serving (2 lamb roll slices with ¹/₄ cup sauce) provides: 3¹/₂ Proteins, 35 Optional Calories.

Per serving: 187 Calories, 6 g Total Fat, 2 g Saturated Fat, 84 mg Cholesterol, 271 mg Sodium, 3 g Total Carbohydrate, 0 g Dietary Fiber, 28 g Protein, 80 mg Calcium.

One cup broth provides: 20 Optional Calories.

Per serving: 20 Calories, 0 g Total Fat, 0 g Saturated Fat, 0 mg Cholesterol, 70 mg Sodium, 0 g Total Carbohydrate, 0 g Dietary Fiber, 5 g Protein, 0 mg Calcium.

LAMB WITH PLUMS

Makes 4 servings

Meat cooked with fruit is traditional in British and German cuisine.

Four 5-ounce lean lamb chops
  (1" thick)
$^1/_2$ teaspoon freshly ground
  black pepper
2 medium onions, chopped
1 garlic clove, chopped
4 large red plums, pitted and
  thinly sliced
4 fluid ounces ($^1/_2$ cup) dry red
  wine

$^1/_4$ cup low-sodium chicken broth
1 teaspoon granulated sugar
Pinch salt
Pinch cinnamon
Pinch ground nutmeg
1 teaspoon cornstarch, dissolved in
  1 tablespoon cold water

1. Preheat broiler. Spray rack in broiler pan with nonstick cooking spray.
2. To prepare lamb, with sharp knife, make several slashes about $^1/_8$" deep and
   $^1/_2$" apart around edge of chops. Place chops onto prepared rack in broiler pan;
   sprinkle with pepper. Broil chops 4" from heat, turning once, 8–11 minutes,
   until cooked through. Transfer 1 chop to each of 4 plates; cover to keep warm.
3. Meanwhile, in medium nonstick skillet, cook onions over medium heat,
   stirring frequently, 6–7 minutes, until lightly browned. Add garlic; cook,
   stirring frequently, 2 minutes.
4. Add all but 4 plum slices, the wine, broth, sugar, salt, cinnamon and nutmeg
   to onion mixture; bring liquid to a boil. Reduce heat to low; simmer, covered, 15 minutes, until onions and plums are very tender.
5. Place food mill or coarse sieve over medium bowl; pass sauce through food mill
   or strain through sieve, pressing with back of wooden spoon to force as much
   mixture through sieve as possible. Return purée to skillet; discard solids.
6. Add dissolved cornstarch, reserved plum slices and any accumulated liquid
   on platter to purée; cook over low heat, stirring constantly, 3 minutes, until
   mixture is thickened. Pour sauce over chops and serve.

Serving (1 lamb chop with $^1/_4$ cup sauce) provides: 1 Fruit, $^1/_2$ Vegetable,
3 Proteins, 35 Optional Calories.

Per serving: 290 Calories, 9 g Total Fat, 3 g Saturated Fat,
81 mg Cholesterol, 115 mg Sodium, 20 g Total Carbohydrate,
3 g Dietary Fiber, 27 g Protein, 36 mg Calcium.

MOROCCAN LAMB TAGINE

Makes 4 servings

For an authentic presentation, serve this Moroccan stew with couscous.

2 teaspoons vegetable oil
10 ounces boneless lean loin or
    leg of lamb, cut into
    1" cubes
2 medium onions, chopped
2 medium celery stalks,
    sliced
4 garlic cloves, minced
1 1/2 teaspoons ground cumin
1/2 teaspoon freshly ground
    black pepper

2 cups canned whole Italian
    tomatoes (no salt added),
    coarsely chopped (reserve juice)
1/4 cup minced fresh flat-leaf
    parsley
One 1" cinnamon stick
1 bay leaf
2 medium carrots, cut into
    1" chunks
2 cups cubed pared butternut
    squash
1 cup sliced parsnips

1. In large pot or Dutch oven, heat oil; add lamb. Cook over medium heat, stirring frequently, 8–10 minutes, until lamb is browned on all sides and cooked through. Remove lamb from pot; set aside.
2. In same pot, cook onions and celery over medium heat, stirring frequently, 3–5 minutes, until onions are softened. Add garlic, cumin and pepper; cook, stirring frequently, 2 minutes.
3. Add tomatoes with juice, parsley, cinnamon, bay leaf, 1/2 cup water and lamb to onion mixture; bring liquid to a boil. Reduce heat to low; simmer, stirring occasionally, 1–1 1/2 hours, until lamb is tender. Add carrots, squash and parsnips; simmer 30 minutes, until vegetables are tender. Remove and discard cinnamon stick and bay leaf. Divide evenly among 4 plates and serve.

Serving (1 1/4 cups) provides: 1/2 Fat, 2 3/4 Vegetables, 2 Proteins, 1 Bread.

Per serving: 253 Calories, 7 g Total Fat, 2 g Saturated Fat, 47 mg Cholesterol, 285 mg Sodium, 31 g Total Carbohydrate, 7 g Dietary Fiber, 19 g Protein, 137 mg Calcium.

LAMB STEW

Makes 4 servings

2 teaspoons vegetable oil
2 cups baby carrots or 2 medium
   carrots, cut into 1" chunks
2 medium onions, cut into
   8 wedges each
1 garlic clove, minced
15 ounces boneless lean loin or
   leg of lamb, cut into $^1/_2$" cubes
1 cup low-sodium chicken broth
1 cup low-sodium beef broth
1 bay leaf
$^1/_2$ teaspoon dried rosemary
   leaves, crumbled
$^1/_2$ teaspoon dried thyme leaves

$^1/_2$ teaspoon dried marjoram
$^1/_4$ teaspoon salt
$^1/_4$ teaspoon freshly ground black
   pepper
10 ounces red potatoes, pared and
   cut into 1" chunks
4 medium celery stalks, cut into
   1" chunks
1 medium white turnip, pared and
   cut into 1" chunks
1 tablespoon red wine vinegar
2 teaspoons all-purpose flour
1 cup fresh or thawed frozen green
   peas

1. In large nonstick saucepan, heat 1 teaspoon of the oil; add carrots and onions. Cook over medium heat, stirring frequently, 8–10 minutes, until onions are golden brown. Add garlic; cook, stirring frequently, 2 minutes. With slotted spoon, remove onion mixture from saucepan; set aside.
2. In same saucepan, heat remaining 1 teaspoon oil; add lamb. Cook over medium heat, stirring frequently, 8–10 minutes, until lamb is browned on all sides and cooked through.
3. Add chicken and beef broths, bay leaf, rosemary, thyme, marjoram, salt and pepper; bring liquid to a boil. Reduce heat to low; simmer, covered, 45 minutes, until lamb is slightly tender.
4. Add potatoes, celery and turnip to lamb mixture; simmer, covered, 20 minutes, until lamb and vegetables are tender.
5. In small bowl, combine vinegar, flour and $^1/_4$ cup water, stirring until flour is dissolved; stir into lamb mixture. Add peas; simmer, uncovered, stirring occasionally, 10 minutes, until peas are tender and liquid is slightly thickened. Remove and discard bay leaf. Divide evenly among 4 bowls and serve.

Serving ($1^1/_2$ cups) provides: $^1/_2$ Fat, $2^1/_2$ Vegetables, 3 Proteins, 1 Bread, 15 Optional Calories.

Per serving: 340 Calories, 10 g Total Fat, 3 g Saturated Fat, 70 mg Cholesterol, 320 mg Sodium, 34 g Total Carbohydrate, 7 g Dietary Fiber, 30 g Protein, 87 mg Calcium.

LANCASHIRE HOT POT

Makes 4 servings

This classic dish is similar to Irish Stew, but it combines kidneys and oysters with the lamb for a deliciously different flavor. If kidneys are difficult to find or not to your liking, omit them and increase the amount of lamb to 12 ounces.

1 pound 14 ounces red potatoes, pared and cut into $1/4$" slices
8 ounces boneless lean leg of lamb, cut into 1" chunks
4 ounces lamb kidneys, diced
$1/2$ teaspoon salt
$1/2$ teaspoon freshly ground black pepper
6 medium oysters, shucked and halved (reserve liquid)

4 medium onions, thinly sliced
2 cups thinly sliced mushrooms
1 bay leaf
$1/2$ cup low-sodium chicken broth
$1/2$ cup low-sodium beef broth
$1/4$ cup minced fresh flat-leaf parsley, to garnish

1. Preheat oven to 350° F. Spray 2-quart casserole with nonstick cooking spray.
2. Line bottom of prepared casserole with one third of the potato slices, overlapping slices as necessary. Top potato slices evenly with half of the lamb and half of the kidneys; sprinkle evenly with pinch *each* of the salt and pepper. Top evenly with half of the oysters, half of the onions and 1 cup of the mushrooms; sprinkle evenly with another pinch *each* of the salt and pepper. Repeat layers; tuck bay leaf into mixture.
3. Carefully pour chicken and beef broths evenly over mixture. Top evenly with remaining potato slices; sprinkle evenly with remaining salt and pepper. Bake 2 hours, until lamb is very tender and potato topping is golden brown. Remove and discard bay leaf. Divide evenly among 4 plates, sprinkle with parsley and serve.

Serving ($1/4$ of stew) provides: 2 Vegetables, $2 1/2$ Proteins, $1 1/2$ Breads, 5 Optional Calories.

Per serving: 316 Calories, 5 g Total Fat, 1 g Saturated Fat, 140 mg Cholesterol, 412 mg Sodium, 45 g Total Carbohydrate, 5 g Dietary Fiber, 24 g Protein, 44 mg Calcium.

SHISH KABOB

Makes 4 servings

If you use bamboo skewers in place of metal ones, soak them in water for 15 minutes before threading the meat and vegetables onto them; this will help prevent the skewers from burning during cooking. Serve kabobs with rice, couscous or a rice salad.

1 tablespoon + 1 teaspoon olive oil
1 tablespoon fresh lemon juice
4 garlic cloves, crushed
1/2 teaspoon freshly ground
  black pepper
1/2 teaspoon dried oregano
Pinch cinnamon
15 ounces boneless lean leg of
  lamb, cut into 1" cubes

2 cups pearl onions
2 cups whole medium mushrooms,
  woody ends trimmed
1 medium red or yellow bell pepper,
  cut into 1" squares
4 small plum tomatoes
1/2 teaspoon salt
1 lemon, cut into wedges

1. To prepare marinade, in gallon-size sealable plastic bag, combine oil, juice, garlic, black pepper, oregano and cinnamon; add lamb. Seal bag, squeezing out air; turn to coat lamb. Refrigerate 2 hours or overnight, turning bag occasionally.
2. Spray rack in broiler pan with nonstick cooking spray and preheat broiler, or preheat outdoor barbecue grill according to manufacturer's directions.
3. Add onions, mushrooms, bell pepper and tomatoes to lamb mixture; turn to coat.
4. Drain and discard marinade. Alternating ingredients, onto 4 long metal skewers, thread an equal amount of lamb and vegetables; grill over hot coals or place onto prepared rack in broiler pan and broil 4" from heat, turning as needed, 6–8 minutes, until lamb is cooked through and vegetables are lightly browned.
5. Transfer kabobs to each of 4 plates; sprinkle evenly with salt. Serve with lemon wedges.

Serving (1 skewer) provides: 3 Vegetables, 3 Proteins, 40 Optional Calories.

Per serving: 245 Calories, 9 g Total Fat, 3 g Saturated Fat, 76 mg Cholesterol, 346 mg Sodium, 16 g Total Carbohydrate, 1 g Dietary Fiber, 26 g Protein, 69 mg Calcium.

Lamb Shanks with Lentils and Spinach

Makes 4 servings

Ask the butcher to cut the shanks into serving-size portions for you.

2 pounds lean lamb shanks, cut into 4 equal pieces*
4 medium onions, chopped
2 large garlic cloves, minced
2 cups stewed tomatoes, chopped
$^1/_2$ cup low-sodium chicken broth
6 ounces lentils, rinsed and drained

1 large bay leaf
$^1/_2$ teaspoon dried oregano
$^1/_2$ teaspoon freshly ground black pepper
One 10-ounce package thawed frozen chopped spinach, thoroughly drained and squeezed dry

1. Preheat oven to 450° F.
2. Place lamb in a single layer into small roasting pan; roast 20–30 minutes, until browned. Remove lamb from oven; reduce oven temperature to 325° F.
3. Add onions and garlic to lamb; roast, stirring once, 20–30 minutes, until vegetables are lightly browned.
4. Add tomatoes and broth to lamb mixture; bake, covered, 1 hour, until lamb is tender.
5. Meanwhile, in medium ovenproof saucepan, bring 2 cups water to a boil; add lentils. Reduce heat to low; simmer, covered, 10 minutes, until lentils begin to soften.
6. Add bay leaf, oregano, pepper and lamb mixture to lentil mixture; bake, covered, 1 hour, until lamb and lentils are very tender. Remove from oven.
7. Add spinach to lamb mixture; bake, covered, 15 minutes. Remove and discard bay leaf. Divide evenly among 4 plates and serve.

Serving (1 lamb shank piece with $^3/_4$ cup lentil mixture) provides:
3 Vegetables, 3 Proteins, 2 Breads, 5 Optional Calories.

Per serving: 371 Calories, 5 g Total Fat, 2 g Saturated Fat, 78 mg Cholesterol, 488 mg Sodium, 44 g Total Carbohydrate, 11 g Dietary Fiber, 41 g Protein, 182 mg Calcium.

* 2 pounds lamb shanks will yield about 12 ounces boned cooked lamb.

SWEDISH LAMB SHANKS

Makes 4 servings

2 pounds lean lamb shanks, cut
   into 4 equal pieces*
2 medium onions, thinly sliced
$^1/_2$ medium carrot, julienned
2 garlic cloves, minced
$^1/_2$ cup low-sodium chicken broth
$^1/_2$ cup brewed coffee

$^1/_2$ teaspoon salt
$^1/_4$ teaspoon freshly ground black
   pepper
$^1/_4$ cup nonfat cream cheese
$^1/_4$ cup skim milk
1 teaspoon cornstarch, dissolved in
   2 teaspoons cold water

1. Preheat oven to 425° F. Spray small roasting pan with nonstick cooking spray.
2. Place lamb in a single layer into prepared roasting pan; roast 45 minutes, until well browned. Remove from oven; reduce oven temperature to 350° F.
3. Add onions, carrot and garlic to browned lamb; bake, covered, stirring once, 30 minutes, until vegetables are tender.
4. Add broth, coffee, salt and pepper to lamb mixture; stir, scraping up browned bits from bottom of pan. Bake, covered, basting lamb several times with pan juices, 30 minutes, until lamb is falling off bone.
5. Meanwhile, in blender or food processor, combine cream cheese and milk; purée until smooth. Set aside.
6. With slotted spoon, transfer lamb and vegetables to serving platter, cover.
7. To prepare sauce, place medium sieve over medium bowl. Strain pan juices through sieve, reserving liquid; discard solids. Let liquid stand 15–20 minutes, until fat accumulates on top; with paper towels or large spoon, remove fat.
8. Transfer liquid to small saucepan; bring just to a boil. Reduce heat to low; stir in dissolved cornstarch. Continuing to stir, cook 2 minutes, until liquid is slightly thickened; remove from heat. With wire whisk, blend in reserved cream cheese mixture. Pour sauce over lamb and vegetables. Divide evenly among 4 plates and serve.

Serving (3 ounces lamb with $^1/_4$ of vegetables, $^1/_3$ cup sauce) provides:
$^3/_4$ Vegetable, 3 Proteins, 25 Optional Calories.

Per serving: 188 Calories, 5 g Total Fat, 1 g Saturated Fat,
80 mg Cholesterol, 459 mg Sodium, 8 g Total Carbohydrate,
1 g Dietary Fiber, 28 g Protein, 89 mg Calcium.

* *Two pounds lamb shanks will yield about 12 ounces boned cooked lamb.*

Braised Lamb Shanks

Makes 4 servings

Serve with couscous or rice pilaf to soak up the spicy sauce.

2 teaspoons curry powder
$^1/_2$ teaspoon salt
$^1/_2$ teaspoon freshly ground
   black pepper
$^1/_2$ teaspoon caraway seeds, crushed
$^1/_2$ teaspoon ground coriander
$^1/_4$ teaspoon cinnamon
$^1/_4$ teaspoon ground red pepper
Pinch ground allspice
2 pounds lean lamb shanks, cut
   into 4 equal pieces*

4 medium onions, thinly sliced
1 medium green bell pepper, diced
1 medium red bell pepper, diced
1 large clove garlic, minced
2 cups low-sodium chicken broth
2 tablespoons raisins, chopped
6 dried apricot halves, slivered
1 tablespoon tomato paste
   (no salt added), dissolved in
   $^1/_2$ cup hot water

1. Preheat oven to 425° F. Spray 2-quart casserole with nonstick cooking spray.
2. In small bowl, combine curry powder, salt, black pepper, caraway seeds, coriander, cinnamon, ground red pepper and allspice; rub 1 tablespoon seasoning mixture into lamb shanks. Place lamb in a single layer into prepared casserole; spray lightly with nonstick spray. Roast lamb 30 minutes, until lightly browned. Remove lamb from casserole; set aside. Reduce oven temperature to 375° F.
3. In same casserole, combine onions, green and red bell peppers and garlic. Sprinkle vegetable mixture with remaining seasoning mixture; toss until evenly coated. Roast 10 minutes, until vegetables are softened. Remove from oven; reduce oven temperature to 300° F.
4. Add broth, raisins, apricots, dissolved tomato paste and browned lamb to vegetable mixture; spoon some of the vegetables over lamb. Bake, covered, 2 hours, until lamb is cooked through and falling off bone. Divide evenly among 4 plates and serve.

Serving (3 ounces lamb, 1 cup vegetables) provides: $^1/_2$ Fruit, $2^1/_4$ Vegetables, 3 Proteins, 10 Optional Calories.

Per serving: 234 Calories, 6 g Total Fat, 2 g Saturated Fat, 78 mg Cholesterol, 429 mg Sodium, 21 g Total Carbohydrate, 4 g Dietary Fiber, 28 g Protein, 62 mg Calcium.

* 2 pounds lamb shanks will yield about 12 ounces boned cooked lamb.

CASSOULET

Makes 8 servings

The heartiest of winter casseroles, this is an ancient French classic. Even this lightened version is so filling you won't need anything but a crusty roll and a small salad to complete the meal—and a glass of crisp, dry white wine, of course.

4^1/$_2$ ounces dried white beans

1 pound 8 ounces lean lamb shanks†

One 12-ounce turkey thigh, skinned‡

6 medium onions, chopped

2 medium carrots, chopped

2 medium celery stalks, minced

4 large garlic cloves, minced

4 fluid ounces (^{1}/$_2$ cup) dry white wine

^{1}/$_2$ cup tomato sauce (no salt added)

3 ounces smoked turkey sausage, cut into ^{1}/$_2$" slices

^{1}/$_4$ cup minced fresh flat-leaf parsley

1 large bay leaf

^{1}/$_2$ teaspoon dried thyme leaves

^{1}/$_4$ teaspoon freshly ground black pepper, or to taste

3 tablespoons plain dried bread crumbs

1. Place beans into medium bowl; add cold water to cover. Let stand overnight.*
2. Drain beans; discard liquid. In medium saucepan, bring 2 cups water to a boil; add beans. Reduce heat to low; simmer, covered, adding ^{1}/$_4$ cup boiling water at a time if mixture begins to stick, 1 hour, until beans are tender. Remove from heat. Drain beans; set aside.
3. Meanwhile, preheat oven to 425° F.
4. Place lamb and turkey into 1^1/$_2$-quart casserole; roast 50–60 minutes, until browned. Remove meat from casserole; set aside. Wipe casserole clean; reduce oven temperature to 350° F.
5. In same casserole, combine onions, carrots, celery and garlic; roast 40–45 minutes, stirring once, until onions are golden brown. Reduce oven temperature to 325° F.

   If you prefer to quick-soak the beans, combine the beans and enough cold water to cover in a large saucepan. Bring to a boil over high heat; boil 2 minutes. Remove from heat; let stand 1 hour, covered. Proceed with step 2.

   †1 pound 8 ounces lamb shanks will yield about 9 ounces boned cooked lamb.

   ‡A 12-ounce turkey thigh will yield about 6 ounces skinned and boned cooked turkey.

6. Add wine, tomato sauce, sausage, parsley, bay leaf, thyme, pepper, beans and meat to vegetable mixture; toss gently to combine. Bake, covered, 2 hours, until meat is cooked through and falling off bone. Increase oven temperature to 375° F.
7. Remove meat from casserole; remove and discard bones. Cut meat into bite-size pieces; stir into bean mixture. Remove and discard bay leaf. Sprinkle evenly with bread crumbs; bake 15 minutes, until mixture is bubbling and topping is browned. Divide evenly among 8 plates and serve.

Serving (1 cup) provides: $3^3/4$ Vegetables, 3 Proteins, 25 Optional Calories.

Per serving: 226 Calories, 4 g Total Fat, 1 g Saturated Fat, 60 mg Cholesterol, 229 mg Sodium, 22 g Total Carbohydrate, 4 g Dietary Fiber, 22 g Protein, 87 mg Calcium.

GREEK LAMB BURGERS

Makes 4 servings

Topped with a spoonful of yogurt and slices of cool cucumber, these scrumptious burgers are a little taste of Greece!

15 ounces lean ground lamb	2 garlic cloves, minced
12 large kalamata olives, pitted and chopped	$1/4$ teaspoon salt
$1^1/2$ ounces feta cheese, crumbled	$1/4$ teaspoon freshly ground black pepper
2 tablespoons minced fresh mint leaves	Two 2-ounce whole-wheat pitas, halved to form 4 pockets
2 tablespoons minced fresh flat-leaf parsley	$1/2$ cup plain nonfat yogurt
	$1/2$ medium cucumber, thinly sliced

1. Spray rack in broiler pan with nonstick cooking spray; preheat broiler.
2. In medium bowl, combine lamb, olives, cheese, mint, parsley, garlic, salt and pepper; form into 4 equal patties.
3. Place patties onto prepared rack in broiler pan; broil 4" from heat, turning once, 14 minutes, until cooked through.
4. Place each burger into 1 pita pocket; top each burger with 2 tablespoons of the yogurt and one fourth of the cucumber slices, and serve.

Serving (1 filled pita pocket) provides: $1/2$ Fat, $1/4$ Vegetable, $3^1/2$ Proteins, 1 Bread, 15 Optional Calories.

Per serving: 354 Calories, 18 g Total Fat, 6 g Saturated Fat, 80 mg Cholesterol, 972 mg Sodium, 21 g Total Carbohydrate, 2 g Dietary Fiber, 28 g Protein, 147 mg Calcium.

Lamb Curry with Raisins, Figs and Apricots

Makes 4 servings

The sweetness of the fruit is balanced by the heat of the jalapeño pepper in this flavorful curry dish. Serve with rice or couscous.

15 ounces lean ground lamb
2 teaspoons vegetable oil
2 medium onions, chopped
4 large garlic cloves, minced
$^1/_2$ medium jalapeño pepper, seeded, deveined and minced, or to taste (wear gloves to prevent irritation)
1 teaspoon paprika
$^1/_2$ teaspoon cinnamon

$1^1/_2$ cups low-sodium beef broth
6 dried apricot halves, coarsely chopped
2 large dried figs, halved
2 tablespoons golden raisins
1 tablespoon chopped crystallized ginger
1 teaspoon ground coriander
$^1/_2$ teaspoon freshly ground black pepper

1. In large nonstick saucepan, cook lamb, stirring to break up meat, 4–5 minutes, until no longer pink. Remove lamb from saucepan; set aside.
2. In same saucepan, heat oil; add onions. Cook over medium heat, stirring frequently, 3–5 minutes, until onions are softened. Add garlic, jalapeño pepper, paprika and cinnamon; cook, stirring frequently, 1–2 minutes, until fragrant.
3. Add broth, apricots, figs, raisins, ginger and lamb to onion mixture; bring liquid to a boil. Reduce heat to low; simmer, stirring occasionally, 15 minutes, until fruits are tender and flavors are blended. Stir in coriander and pepper. Divide evenly among 4 plates and serve.

Serving (1 cup) provides: $^1/_2$ Fat, 1 Fruit, $^3/_4$ Vegetable, 3 Proteins, 20 Optional Calories.

Per serving: 300 Calories, 12 g Total Fat, 4 g Saturated Fat, 70 mg Cholesterol, 110 mg Sodium, 23 g Total Carbohydrate, 2 g Dietary Fiber, 25 g Protein, 65 mg Calcium.

Koftah Curry

Makes 4 servings

Serve these delicious egg-shaped meatballs in their spicy, creamy sauce on a bed of rice pilaf. For lovely canapés or hors d'oeuvres, use slivered almonds in place of the whole almonds, make the meatballs smaller and serve with the sauce for dipping.

$^1/_2$ ounce blanched shelled almonds (about 12 almonds)	$^1/_2$ teaspoon mild or hot curry powder
14 ounces lean ground lamb	Pinch cinnamon
2 ounces drained cooked chick-peas (garbanzo beans), mashed	Pinch ground red pepper
	$^1/_2$ teaspoon vegetable oil
1 medium onion, minced	2 garlic cloves, minced
$^1/_4$ cup minced fresh cilantro	$^1/_4$ teaspoon ground cumin
1 teaspoon grated pared fresh ginger root	$^1/_4$ teaspoon ground turmeric
	$^1/_2$ cup low-sodium chicken broth
$^3/_4$ teaspoon salt	$^1/_2$ cup plain nonfat yogurt
	1 teaspoon cornstarch

1. Place almonds into small heat-resistant bowl; add boiling water to cover. Let stand 5 minutes.
2. Meanwhile, in medium bowl, combine lamb, chick-peas, half of the onion, 2 tablespoons of the cilantro, the ginger, $^1/_2$ teaspoon of the salt, the curry powder, cinnamon and pepper. Divide lamb mixture into 12 equal portions; shape each portion into a 3" patty.
3. Drain almonds, discarding liquid; place 1 almond onto center of each lamb patty. Fold patties around almonds to enclose, forming 12 egg-shaped meatballs.
4. Spray medium nonstick skillet with nonstick cooking spray; heat. Add meatballs; cook over medium heat, turning as needed, 8–10 minutes, until browned on all sides. Remove meatballs from skillet; set aside.
5. To prepare sauce, in same skillet, heat oil; add remaining onion. Cook over medium heat, stirring frequently, 8–10 minutes, until onion is golden brown. Reduce heat to low; add garlic, cumin and turmeric. Cook, stirring constantly, 3 minutes, until onion is evenly coated (do not burn). Remove from heat; set aside.
6. In small bowl, with wire whisk, combine broth, yogurt, cornstarch, remaining 2 tablespoons cilantro and remaining $^1/_4$ teaspoon salt, blending until cornstarch is dissolved; stir into onion mixture.

7. Return skillet to heat; bring liquid to a boil. Reduce heat to low; add meatballs. Simmer, basting meatballs occasionally with sauce, 10 minutes, until meatballs are cooked through and flavors are blended. Divide evenly among 4 plates and serve.

Serving (3 meatballs with ¹/₄ cup sauce) provides: ¹/₄ Fat, ¹/₄ Vegetable, 3 Proteins, 35 Optional Calories.

Per serving: 253 Calories, 13 g Total Fat, 4 g Saturated Fat, 66 mg Cholesterol, 522 mg Sodium, 10 g Total Carbohydrate, 1 g Dietary Fiber, 22 g Protein, 100 mg Calcium.

LAMB LOAF WITH TZATZIKI SAUCE

Makes 8 servings

The sauce for this loaf is heaven for garlic lovers; if you'd prefer, the amount of garlic may be reduced, or omitted entirely.

$^1/_2$ medium cucumber, pared, seeded and minced

$1^1/_2$ teaspoons salt

1 pound 14 ounces lean ground lamb

$^1/_2$ cup + 1 tablespoon plain dried bread crumbs

$1^1/_4$ cups plain nonfat yogurt

2 medium onions, chopped

2 medium celery stalks, chopped

$^1/_2$ medium red bell pepper, chopped

$^1/_4$ cup tomato sauce (no salt added)

1 teaspoon dried oregano

$^3/_4$ teaspoon freshly ground black pepper

$^1/_4$ cup minced fresh mint leaves

2 garlic cloves, crushed

1. Preheat oven to 350° F. Spray 8" × 4" loaf pan with nonstick cooking spray.
2. Set colander into sink; add cucumber and $^1/_2$ teaspoon of the salt, tossing to combine. Place plate directly onto cucumber mixture; weight down with 1-pound can. Let stand 1 hour to drain.
3. Meanwhile, to prepare lamb loaf, in large bowl, combine lamb and bread crumbs; set aside.
4. In food processor or blender, combine $^1/_2$ cup of the yogurt, the onions, celery, bell pepper, tomato sauce, oregano, $^1/_2$ teaspoon of the black pepper and remaining 1 teaspoon salt; purée until almost smooth.
5. Add yogurt mixture to lamb mixture; mix well. Transfer lamb mixture to prepared loaf pan, pressing down firmly; bake 1 hour.
6. Rinse cucumber under running cold water; transfer to paper towels to drain.
7. To prepare sauce, in small bowl, combine mint, garlic, drained cucumber, remaining $^3/_4$ cup yogurt and remaining $^1/_4$ teaspoon black pepper; let stand 30 minutes.
8. Remove loaf from oven; let stand 15 minutes. Cut loaf into 8 equal slices; serve each slice topped with one eighth of the sauce.

Serving (1 slice lamb loaf with 2 tablespoons sauce) provides:
$^3/_4$ Vegetable, 3 Proteins, $^1/_4$ Bread, 30 Optional Calories.

Per serving: 247 Calories, 10 g Total Fat, 4 g Saturated Fat, 71 mg Cholesterol, 488 mg Sodium, 12 g Total Carbohydrate, 1 g Dietary Fiber, 25 g Protein, 118 mg Calcium.

STUFFED ZUCCHINI

Makes 4 servings

These zucchini "boats" are a wonderful way to make use of excess zucchini.

4 medium zucchini, halved lengthwise	$^1/_3$ cup + 2 teaspoons minced fresh flat-leaf parsley
2 teaspoons olive oil	$1^1/_2$ teaspoons dried oregano
1 medium onion, chopped	1 teaspoon dried thyme leaves
1 medium red bell pepper, chopped	$^1/_2$ teaspoon cinnamon
1 garlic clove, minced	$^1/_4$ teaspoon ground cloves
15 ounces lean ground lamb	Pinch salt
1 cup canned crushed tomatoes (no salt added)	Pinch freshly ground black pepper

1. Preheat oven to 375° F. Spray 2-quart rectangular baking dish with nonstick cooking spray.
2. With grapefruit spoon or paring knife, remove pulp from zucchini, leaving $^1/_2$" shells. Chop pulp; set shells and pulp aside.
3. Fill large nonstick skillet with $^1/_2$" water; add zucchini shells, cut-side down. Bring liquid to a boil; cook 5 minutes, until shells are tender but still hold their shape. With slotted spoon, transfer shells to paper towels, cut-side down, to drain. Discard water and wipe skillet dry.
4. In same skillet, heat oil; add onion, bell pepper and garlic. Cook over medium heat, stirring frequently, 6–7 minutes, until onion is lightly browned. Add lamb; cook, stirring to break up meat, 4–5 minutes, until no longer pink. Add chopped zucchini pulp; cook, stirring frequently, 10 minutes, until zucchini is tender.
5. Transfer lamb mixture to large bowl; stir in tomatoes, $^1/_4$ cup of the parsley, the oregano, thyme, cinnamon and cloves.
6. Place zucchini shells, cut-side up, into prepared baking dish; sprinkle evenly with salt and black pepper. Divide lamb mixture evenly among zucchini shells; bake 25–30 minutes, until filling is golden brown and heated through. Place 2 zucchini halves on each of 4 plates, sprinkle with remaining 2 tablespoons parsley and serve.

Serving (2 stuffed zucchini halves) provides: $^1/_2$ Fat, $3^1/_4$ Vegetables, 3 Proteins.

Per serving: 258 Calories, 13 g Total Fat, 4 g Saturated Fat, 70 mg Cholesterol, 126 mg Sodium, 12 g Total Carbohydrate, 2 g Dietary Fiber, 24 g Protein, 89 mg Calcium.

PAPUTSAKIA (GREEK STUFFED EGGPLANT)

Makes 4 servings

Paputsakia means "little shoes" in Greek, and that is what these individual casseroles look like . . . you can even eat the container! Serve with a salad of bitter greens and some crusty bread.

Two 1-pound eggplants
1¹/₂ teaspoons salt
1 teaspoon olive oil
2¹/₂ medium onions, minced
10 ounces lean ground lamb
1 cup cooked long-grain rice
¹/₂ cup tomato sauce
  (no salt added)
1 tablespoon minced fresh basil,
  or ¹/₂ teaspoon dried
¹/₄ teaspoon freshly ground
  black pepper

2 tablespoons all-purpose flour
1 cup hot skim milk
1 small bay leaf
Pinch ground nutmeg
¹/₂ teaspoon grated lemon zest*
2 teaspoons fresh lemon juice
1¹/₂ ounces part-skim mozzarella
  cheese, shredded
1 tablespoon + 1 teaspoon plain
  dried bread crumbs

1. Cut eggplants in half lengthwise. With sharp knife, lightly score cut sides of eggplants at ¹/₂" intervals, creating a crisscross pattern; sprinkle evenly with 1 teaspoon of the salt. Let stand 1 hour.
2. Preheat oven to 375° F. Spray shallow casserole large enough to hold eggplant halves in a single layer or 4 individual gratin dishes with nonstick cooking spray.
3. With paper towels, pat eggplants until dry; with grapefruit spoon or paring knife, remove pulp from eggplants, leaving a ¹/₂" shell. Dice pulp; set shells and pulp aside.
4. In medium nonstick skillet, heat oil; add onions. Cook over medium heat, stirring frequently, 3–5 minutes, until onions are softened. Remove ¹/₄ cup cooked onion from skillet; set aside.
5. Add lamb to cooked onions in skillet; cook, stirring to break up meat, 4–5 minutes, until no longer pink. Remove lamb mixture from skillet; set aside.

---

* The zest of the lemon is the peel without any of the pith (white membrane). To remove zest from lemon, use a zester or the fine side of a vegetable grater.

6. In same skillet, cook diced eggplant pulp over medium heat, stirring frequently, until softened. Remove from heat; stir in rice, tomato sauce, basil, pepper, $^1/_4$ teaspoon of the remaining salt and reserved lamb mixture. Fill each reserved eggplant shell with one-fourth of the lamb mixture; place, stuffed-side up, into prepared casserole or gratin dishes.

7. To prepare sauce, in small nonstick saucepan, combine flour and reserved $^1/_4$ cup cooked onion; cook over low heat, stirring constantly, 2 minutes, until flour is dissolved. With wire whisk, slowly blend in hot milk; add bay leaf, nutmeg and remaining $^1/_4$ teaspoon salt. Cook 5 minutes, continuing to stir, until mixture is thickened and smooth. Stir in zest and juice; remove and discard bay leaf.

8. Spoon sauce evenly over eggplant halves; sprinkle evenly with cheese and bread crumbs. Bake 30–35 minutes, until filling is browned and sauce is bubbling. Place 1 eggplant half on each of 4 plates and serve.

Serving (1 eggplant half) provides: $^1/_4$ Milk, $^1/_4$ Fat, $4^1/_4$ Vegetables, $2^1/_2$ Proteins, $^1/_2$ Bread, 25 Optional Calories.

Per serving: 349 Calories, 10 g Total Fat, 4 g Saturated Fat, 54 mg Cholesterol, 992 mg Sodium, 41 g Total Carbohydrate, 4 g Dietary Fiber, 24 g Protein, 253 mg Calcium.

LAMB COUSCOUS WITH RAISINS AND APPLES

Makes 4 servings

Sweet raisins, a tart apple and savory lamb combine for a most satisfying, easy-to-prepare meal.

$1^1/_4$ cups low-sodium chicken broth
8 ounces couscous
1 teaspoon olive oil
2 medium onions, diced
1 medium red bell pepper, diced
1 small Granny Smith apple, cored and diced

1 garlic clove, minced
8 ounces cooked boneless lean lamb, diced
$^1/_2$ cup raisins
2 teaspoons mild or hot curry powder

1. In medium saucepan, bring broth to a boil. Stir in couscous; remove from heat. Let stand, covered, 5–8 minutes, until all liquid is absorbed.
2. Meanwhile, in medium nonstick skillet, heat oil; add onions, bell pepper, apple and garlic. Cook over medium heat, stirring frequently, 3–5 minutes, until onions are softened.
3. Add lamb, raisins and curry powder to onion mixture; cook, stirring frequently, 2–3 minutes, until heated through. Stir in warm couscous. Divide evenly among 4 plates and serve.

Serving ($^3/_4$ cup) provides: $^1/_4$ Fat, $1^1/_4$ Fruits, 1 Vegetable, 2 Proteins, 2 Breads, 5 Optional Calories.

Per serving: 442 Calories, 8 g Total Fat, 3 g Saturated Fat, 49 mg Cholesterol, 83 mg Sodium, 69 g Total Carbohydrate, 5 g Dietary Fiber, 25 g Protein, 56 mg Calcium.

5

POULTRY

Brunswick Stew • Chicken Stew with Dumplings • Chicken-Vegetable Curry

Braised Chicken with Dried Fruit • Chicken Stew with Wild Mushrooms

Chicken Gumbo • Chicken in the Pot • Chicken Pot Pie with Yogurt-Biscuit Topping

Chicken Enchilada Casserole • Jambalaya • Curried Chicken and Chick-Pea Salad

Chicken, Fig and Walnut Salad • Turkey-Barley Soup • Turkey Thigh Fricassee

Turkey-Bean Enchiladas • Harvest Pie • Turkey Meatloaf • White Chili

Pastitsio • Lentil–Smoked Turkey Soup • Turkey–Sweet Potato Salad

Choucroute Garni • Lentils with Sausage and Greens • Fricasseed Quail

Cornish Hens in "Cream"

BRUNSWICK STEW

Makes 8 servings

An old-fashioned Carolina barbecue always includes a stew like this. The original was made with squirrel, but our version substitutes chicken; if you'd like, try using rabbit instead. Serve the stew with biscuits or corn bread, and a platter of sliced cucumbers or tomatoes on the side.

One 2-pound 4-ounce chicken, skinned and cut into eighths
10 ounces boneless lean beef loin or round, cut into ¹/₂" cubes
2 cups low-sodium chicken broth
4 ounces cooked boneless lean Virginia ham, cut into ¹/₂" cubes
1 tablespoon granulated sugar
1 tablespoon minced fresh basil, or 1 teaspoon dried
8 fresh flat-leaf parsley sprigs
1 bay leaf
4 cups stewed tomatoes (no salt added)

8 ounces cooked red potatoes, peeled and mashed
2 cups thawed frozen baby green lima beans
2 cups fresh or thawed frozen corn kernels
2 medium onions, thinly sliced
2 medium celery stalks, thinly sliced
¹/₂ teaspoon freshly ground black pepper
¹/₂ teaspoon crushed red pepper flakes, or to taste
Pinch salt

1. Place chicken into large pot or Dutch oven; add water to cover. Bring liquid to a boil. Reduce heat to low; simmer 10 minutes, until chicken turns white. Drain chicken; discard liquid.

2. In same pot, combine beef, broth, ham, sugar, basil, parsley, bay leaf and chicken; add enough water to cover half of mixture. Bring liquid to a boil. Reduce heat to low; simmer, covered, 1¹/₂–2 hours, until beef and chicken are cooked through and chicken is falling off bone.

3. With slotted spoon, remove beef, chicken and ham from liquid; set aside to cool.

4. Place medium sieve over medium bowl. Strain liquid through sieve, reserving liquid; discard solids. Let liquid stand 15–20 minutes, until fat accumulates on top; with paper towels or large spoon, remove fat.

5. When chicken is cool enough to handle, remove and discard chicken bones; shred chicken.

6. In same pot, combine tomatoes, potatoes, lima beans, corn, onions, celery and reserved liquid; bring liquid to a boil. Reduce heat to low; simmer, stirring occasionally, 30 minutes, until vegetables are tender and mixture is slightly thickened.

7. Add black pepper, pepper flakes, salt, shredded chicken, beef and ham; simmer 20 minutes, until mixture is heated through and flavors are blended. Divide evenly among 8 plates and serve.

Serving (1^1/$_2$ cups) provides: 1^1/$_2$ Vegetables, 3 Proteins, 1^1/$_4$ Breads, 10 Optional Calories.

Per serving: 306 Calories, 6 g Total Fat, 2 g Saturated Fat, 67 mg Cholesterol, 372 mg Sodium, 36 g Total Carbohydrate, 7 g Dietary Fiber, 30 g Protein, 85 mg Calcium.

CHICKEN STEW WITH DUMPLINGS

Makes 4 servings

Few things are as warming on a cold night as chicken with dumplings. Feel free to substitute your favorite fresh herb for the chives.

Stew:
1 pound chicken parts, skinned and cut into 8 equal pieces
1 1/2 cups low-sodium chicken broth
1 cup skim milk
3 medium carrots, cut into 1" chunks
2 medium celery stalks, sliced
1 medium onion, sliced
1/4 cup minced fresh flat-leaf parsley
1 bay leaf
1 teaspoon dried thyme leaves
1/2 teaspoon salt
1/2 teaspoon freshly ground black pepper
1/4 cup all-purpose flour

Dumplings:
2 ounces day-old bread, cut into 1/4"–1/2" cubes
2 tablespoons all-purpose flour
2 tablespoons minced fresh flat-leaf parsley
2 tablespoons skim milk
1 tablespoon minced fresh chives
1 egg white
1 teaspoon vegetable oil
1/2 teaspoon salt
1/4 teaspoon freshly ground black pepper
1/4 teaspoon double-acting baking powder

1. To prepare stew, in large saucepan, combine chicken, broth, milk, carrots, celery, onion, parsley, bay leaf, thyme, salt and pepper; bring liquid to a boil. Reduce heat to low; simmer 30 minutes, until chicken is cooked through and vegetables are tender.
2. With slotted spoon, remove chicken from saucepan; remove and discard bones. Shred chicken; set aside.
3. In small bowl, combine flour and 1/4 cup water, stirring until flour is dissolved. With wire whisk, blend flour mixture into broth mixture; simmer, stirring occasionally, 10 minutes, until slightly thickened. Remove and discard bay leaf.
4. Meanwhile, to prepare dumplings, in medium bowl, combine bread, flour, parsley, milk, chives, egg white, oil, salt, pepper and baking powder; let stand 5 minutes.

5. Transfer dough to work surface; knead 1 minute. Divide dough into 8 equal portions; form each portion into a ball.
6. Transfer shredded chicken to broth mixture; stir to combine. Gently place dough balls onto surface of broth mixture; simmer, covered, turning balls once, 7–8 minutes, until cooked through. Divide evenly among 4 plates and serve.

Serving (1 cup stew with 2 dumplings) provides: $^1/_4$ Milk, $^1/_4$ Fat, 2 Vegetables, 2 Proteins, 1 Bread, 15 Optional Calories.

Per serving: 260 Calories, 5 g Total Fat, 1 g Saturated Fat, 51 mg Cholesterol, 843 mg Sodium, 31 g Total Carbohydrate, 4 g Dietary Fiber, 23 g Protein, 186 mg Calcium.

CHICKEN-VEGETABLE CURRY

Makes 4 servings

This fragrant curry is similar to those found all over India.

3 garlic cloves, peeled
1 tablespoon sliced pared fresh
  ginger root
2 teaspoons vegetable oil
1 medium onion, thickly sliced
1 tablespoon mild or hot
  curry powder
1 teaspoon ground cumin
$1/4$ teaspoon cinnamon
1 pound chicken parts, skinned
  and cut into 8 equal pieces

1 cup low-sodium chicken broth
1 cup canned crushed tomatoes
  (no salt added)
5 ounces all-purpose potato,
  pared and cut into chunks
2 cups okra, cut into 1" chunks
Pinch salt
Pinch freshly ground black
  pepper, or to taste

1. In food processor, combine garlic, ginger and 3 tablespoons water; purée until smooth. Set aside.
2. In large nonstick saucepan, heat oil; add onion, curry powder, cumin and cinnamon. Cook over medium heat, stirring frequently, 3–5 minutes, until onion is softened. Add chicken; cook, turning chicken as needed, until browned on all sides.
3. Add garlic mixture to chicken mixture; cook, stirring constantly, 1 minute, until thoroughly combined. Add broth and tomatoes; bring liquid to a boil. Reduce heat to low; simmer, covered, 20 minutes, until chicken is partially cooked through. Add potato, okra, salt and pepper; simmer, covered, stirring occasionally, 15–20 minutes, until chicken and potatoes are cooked through. Divide evenly among 4 plates and serve.

Serving (1$1/2$ cups) provides: $1/2$ Fat, 1$3/4$ Vegetables, 2 Proteins, $1/4$ Bread, 5 Optional Calories.

Per serving: 189 Calories, 6 g Total Fat, 1 g Saturated Fat, 50 mg Cholesterol, 133 mg Sodium, 17 g Total Carbohydrate, 4 g Dietary Fiber, 19 g Protein, 94 mg Calcium.

BRAISED CHICKEN WITH DRIED FRUIT

Makes 4 servings

2 teaspoons olive oil
1¹/₂ medium onions, thinly sliced
1 teaspoon paprika
1 teaspoon minced pared fresh
    ginger root
¹/₂ teaspoon ground cumin
¹/₄ teaspoon freshly ground black
    pepper

Four 4-ounce chicken legs or
    thighs, skinned
2 cups low-sodium chicken broth
6 dried apricot halves, halved
6 medium pitted prunes, halved
2 tablespoons raisins or dried
    cranberries
Two 4 × ¹/₂" strips lemon zest*
2 teaspoons fresh lemon juice

1. In large pot or Dutch oven, heat oil; add onions. Cook over medium heat, stirring frequently, 3–5 minutes, until onions are softened. Add paprika, ginger, cumin and pepper; cook, stirring constantly, 1 minute, until onions are evenly coated (do not burn).
2. Add chicken, broth, apricots, prunes, raisins and zest to onion mixture; bring liquid to a boil. Reduce heat to low; simmer, stirring occasionally, 45 minutes, until fruits are very tender and chicken is cooked through.
3. With slotted spoon, remove chicken from pot; set aside.
4. Increase heat to high; cook broth mixture, stirring occasionally, 8–10 minutes, until thickened. Stir in juice.
5. Return chicken to pot; turn to coat with broth mixture. Reduce heat to low; simmer until chicken is heated through. Remove and discard zest. Divide evenly among 4 plates and serve.

Serving (2 ounces chicken, ¹/₃ cup broth mixture) provides: ¹/₂ Fat, 1 Fruit, ¹/₂ Vegetable, 2 Proteins, 10 Optional Calories.

Per serving with raisins: 215 Calories, 7 g Total Fat, 2 g Saturated Fat, 68 mg Cholesterol, 134 mg Sodium, 21 g Total Carbohydrate, 2 g Dietary Fiber, 20 g Protein, 41 mg Calcium.

Per serving with cranberries: 213 Calories, 7 g Total Fat, 2 g Saturated Fat, 68 mg Cholesterol, 133 mg Sodium, 20 g Total Carbohydrate, 2 g Dietary Fiber, 20 g Protein, 39 mg Calcium.

* *The zest of the lemon is the peel without any of the pith (white membrane). To remove zest from lemon, use a zester or vegetable peeler.*

CHICKEN STEW WITH WILD MUSHROOMS

Makes 6 servings

Wild mushrooms give this stew a slightly earthy flavor that contrasts well with the delicate chicken. Serve over a bed of pappardelle noodles, with a salad of arugula and watercress.

1 ounce dried porcini mushrooms

1 cup low-sodium chicken broth

4 fluid ounces ($^1/_2$ cup) dry red wine

One 3-pound chicken, skinned and cut into 6 equal pieces

2 teaspoons olive oil

1 medium onion, thinly sliced

2 ounces cooked regular or garlic-seasoned sweet Italian pork sausage, crumbled

2 garlic cloves, minced

$^1/_2$ cup stewed tomatoes (no salt added), pureed

6 large or 10 small Niçoise olives, pitted

1 teaspoon tomato paste (no salt added)

$^1/_2$ teaspoon dried rosemary leaves, crumbled

1. In small bowl, combine mushrooms and $^2/_3$ cup warm water; let stand 30 minutes, until mushrooms are reconstituted.
2. Drain mushrooms, reserving liquid. Rinse mushrooms; slice. Set mushrooms aside.
3. Line medium sieve with coffee filter or double layer of cheesecloth; place over medium nonstick skillet. Pour mushroom liquid through sieve. Reserve liquid; discard solids.
4. Add broth and wine to mushroom liquid; bring to a boil. Add chicken. Reduce heat to low; simmer, covered, turning chicken pieces once, 10 minutes. Remove from heat; set aside.
5. In large nonstick skillet, heat oil; add onion and sausage. Cook over medium heat, stirring frequently, 8–10 minutes, until onion is golden brown. Add garlic; cook, stirring frequently, 2 minutes.
6. Add tomatoes, olives, tomato paste, rosemary, reserved mushrooms and chicken mixture to onion mixture; bring liquid to a boil. Reduce heat to low; simmer, covered, 1 hour, until chicken is cooked through and tender. Transfer chicken to serving platter; cover to keep warm.

7. Increase heat to high; cook tomato mixture, stirring occasionally, 3 minutes, until mixture is slightly thickened. Pour over chicken. Divide evenly among 6 plates and serve.

Serving (1 piece chicken with $^1/_4$ cup tomato mixture) provides: $^1/_2$ Fat, $^1/_2$ Vegetable, 3 Proteins, 20 Optional Calories.

Per serving: 211 Calories, 8 g Total Fat, 2 g Saturated Fat, 74 mg Cholesterol, 320 mg Sodium, 7 g Total Carbohydrate, 2 g Dietary Fiber, 24 g Protein, 40 mg Calcium.

CHICKEN GUMBO

Makes 4 servings

The combination of oil and flour, cooked until deep golden brown, flavors and colors as well as thickens this popular Southern entrée. Do not rush this step or the richness that makes this dish so special will be lost.

2 tablespoons all-purpose flour
1 tablespoon vegetable oil
10 ounces skinless boneless chicken breasts, diced
16 medium scallions, chopped
2 medium celery stalks, chopped
1 medium green bell pepper, chopped
2 garlic cloves, minced
1 1/2 cups low-sodium chicken broth
1 cup okra, cut into 1/2" pieces

1/2 cup canned whole Italian tomatoes (no salt added), chopped (reserve juice)
2 ounces cooked boneless lean Virginia ham, diced
1 bay leaf
1 teaspoon Worcestershire sauce
1/2 teaspoon dried thyme leaves
1/4 teaspoon freshly ground black pepper
2 cups cooked long-grain rice
Hot red pepper sauce, to taste

1. In medium nonstick skillet, combine flour and oil; cook over medium-low heat, stirring constantly, 5–8 minutes, until deep golden brown. Transfer to small heat-resistant bowl; set aside.
2. In same skillet, cook chicken over medium heat, stirring frequently, 4–5 minutes, until browned on all sides and cooked through. Remove from skillet; set aside.
3. In same skillet, combine scallions, celery, bell pepper and garlic; cook over medium heat, stirring frequently, 3–5 minutes, until vegetables are tender. Stir in broth, okra, tomatoes with juice, ham, bay leaf, Worcestershire sauce, thyme and black pepper; bring liquid to a boil. Reduce heat to low; simmer, covered, 10 minutes, until flavors are blended.
4. Add 2 tablespoons hot water to browned flour mixture; stir until smooth. Stir into broth mixture; simmer, covered, stirring occasionally, 15 minutes, until mixture is slightly thickened. Stir in chicken; simmer, stirring frequently, 1–2 minutes, until heated through. Remove and discard bay leaf.
5. Divide rice evenly among 4 bowls; top each with an equal portion of chicken mixture. Serve with pepper sauce.

Serving (1¹/₂ cups chicken mixture with ¹/₂ cup rice) provides: ³/₄ Fat, 2 Vegetables, 2¹/₂ Proteins, 1 Bread, 25 Optional Calories.

Per serving: 323 Calories, 7 g Total Fat, 1 g Saturated Fat, 49 mg Cholesterol, 345 mg Sodium, 41 g Total Carbohydrate, 3 g Dietary Fiber, 25 g Protein, 92 mg Calcium.

CHICKEN IN THE POT

Makes 4 servings

Enjoy this warming stew on a blustery evening for a hearty, filling meal that can be prepared in under an hour.

3 cups low-sodium chicken broth	1 garlic clove, crushed
2 medium onions, cut into 8 wedges each	¹/₂ teaspoon dried thyme leaves
	6 whole black peppercorns
2 medium carrots, cut into 1" chunks	Four 4-ounce chicken thighs, skinned
2 medium celery stalks, cut into 1" chunks	3 ounces wide egg noodles
	1 cup cut green beans (1" pieces)
1 bay leaf	

1. In large pot or Dutch oven, combine broth, onions, carrots, celery, bay leaf, garlic, thyme, peppercorns and 1 cup water; bring to a boil. Reduce heat to low; simmer 20 minutes, until vegetables are tender.
2. Add chicken; simmer 20 minutes, until chicken is cooked through.
3. Add noodles and beans to chicken mixture; simmer, stirring occasionally, 5–7 minutes, until noodles are tender. Remove and discard bay leaf and peppercorns. Divide evenly among 4 plates and serve.

Serving (2 ounces chicken with 1¹/₄ cups broth mixture) provides: 2¹/₄ Vegetables, 2 Proteins, 1 Bread, 15 Optional Calories.

Per serving: 252 Calories, 6 g Total Fat, 2 g Saturated Fat, 91 mg Cholesterol, 198 mg Sodium, 28 g Total Carbohydrate, 4 g Dietary Fiber, 24 g Protein, 73 mg Calcium.

CHICKEN POT PIE WITH YOGURT-BISCUIT TOPPING

Makes 4 servings

Chicken pot pie is a long-time favorite, and this version will remind you of the ones you enjoyed as a child. The biscuit topping, made with yogurt in place of some of the fat, is served up golden brown and steaming hot, just like you remember.

2 $^1/_2$ cups low-sodium chicken broth

3 medium carrots, cut into 1" chunks

2 medium onions, quartered

1 bay leaf

1 teaspoon dried thyme leaves

$^1/_2$ teaspoon freshly ground black pepper

1 cup + 2 tablespoons all-purpose flour

8 ounces skinless boneless cooked chicken breast, shredded

$^1/_2$ cup fresh or thawed frozen green peas

1 teaspoon granulated sugar

1 teaspoon double-acting baking powder

$^1/_4$ teaspoon baking soda

$^1/_4$ teaspoon salt

$^1/_2$ cup plain nonfat yogurt

1 tablespoon + 1 teaspoon vegetable oil

1. Preheat oven to 350° F.
2. To prepare filling, in medium saucepan, combine broth, carrots, onions, bay leaf, thyme and pepper; bring liquid to a boil. Reduce heat to low; simmer 20 minutes, until vegetables are tender.
3. In small bowl, combine 3 tablespoons of the flour and $^1/_4$ cup water, stirring until flour is dissolved. Add $^1/_2$ cup hot broth to flour mixture; with wire whisk, blend until smooth. Stir flour mixture into remaining broth mixture; simmer, stirring frequently, 5 minutes, until mixture is thickened. Stir in chicken and peas; transfer to 9" square baking pan. Remove and discard bay leaf.
4. To prepare topping, in medium bowl, combine the remaining 1 cup minus 1 tablespoon flour, the sugar, baking powder, baking soda and salt. Add yogurt and oil; stir until mixture forms a smooth dough. Divide dough into 4 equal portions. Form each portion into a ball; flatten balls slightly. Place flattened balls onto filling without overlapping dough; bake 30 minutes, until topping is golden brown and filling is bubbling. Divide evenly among 4 plates and serve.

Serving (one-fourth of pie) provides: 1 Fat, 2 Vegetables, 2 Proteins, 1³/₄ Breads, 30 Optional Calories.

Per serving: 364 Calories, 9 g Total Fat, 2 g Saturated Fat, 49 mg Cholesterol, 500 mg Sodium, 46 g Total Carbohydrate, 5 g Dietary Fiber, 27 g Protein, 193 mg Calcium.

CHICKEN ENCHILADA CASSEROLE

Makes 4 servings

This casserole is more like a Mexican lasagna than traditional enchiladas, since the ingredients are layered rather than rolled and placed side by side; it is much easier to make and serve, but is every bit as delicious.

1 teaspoon olive or vegetable oil
2 medium onions, diced
1 medium red bell pepper, diced
1 medium green bell pepper, diced
3 garlic cloves, minced
1 1/2 teaspoons mild or hot chili powder
1/2 teaspoon ground cumin
1/2 teaspoon dried oregano
Pinch ground red pepper

Pinch cinnamon
2 cups canned crushed tomatoes (no salt added)
Six 6" corn tortillas, cut into 1" strips
4 ounces skinless boneless cooked chicken breast, shredded
3 ounces Monterey Jack cheese, shredded

1. Preheat oven to 375° F. Spray 8" square baking pan with nonstick cooking spray.
2. In large nonstick skillet, heat oil; add onions and red and green bell peppers. Cook over medium heat, stirring frequently, 6–7 minutes, until onions are lightly browned. Add garlic, chili powder, cumin, oregano, ground red pepper and cinnamon; cook, stirring frequently, 2 minutes. Add tomatoes; bring mixture to a boil. Reduce heat to low; simmer, stirring occasionally, 20 minutes, until mixture is thickened.
3. Spread one-third of the tomato mixture evenly in prepared pan. Top evenly with half of the tortilla strips and the chicken; spread evenly with half of the remaining tomato mixture. Sprinkle evenly with 1 1/2 ounces of the cheese; top cheese with remaining tortilla strips. Spread evenly with remaining tomato mixture; sprinkle evenly with remaining 1 1/2 ounces cheese. Bake 30 minutes, until lightly browned and bubbling. Divide evenly among 4 plates and serve.

Serving (one-fourth of casserole) provides: 1/4 Fat, 2 1/2 Vegetables, 2 Proteins, 1 1/2 Breads.

Per serving: 282 Calories, 10 g Total Fat, 4 g Saturated Fat, 47 mg Cholesterol, 403 mg Sodium, 31 g Total Carbohydrate, 5 g Dietary Fiber, 18 g Protein, 285 mg Calcium.

JAMBALAYA

Makes 4 servings

2 teaspoons vegetable oil
5 ounces skinless boneless chicken
   thighs, cut into bite-size pieces
2 ounces cooked andouille
   sausage*, sliced
2 medium onions, minced
1 medium celery stalk, minced
$^1/_2$ medium green bell pepper,
   minced
6 ounces long-grain rice
$1^3/_4$ cups low-sodium chicken broth

$^1/_2$ cup whole Italian tomatoes,
   drained and chopped
$^1/_2$ teaspoon dried thyme leaves
$^1/_4$ teaspoon freshly ground black
   pepper
$^1/_4$ teaspoon ground red pepper
5 ounces peeled deveined
   medium shrimp
2 tablespoons minced fresh
   flat-leaf parsley, to garnish

1. In medium nonstick skillet, heat oil; add chicken and sausage. Cook over medium heat, stirring frequently, 4–5 minutes, until chicken is cooked through and lightly browned. Remove from skillet; set aside.
2. In same skillet, combine onions, celery and bell pepper; cook over medium heat, stirring frequently, 6–7 minutes, until onions are lightly browned. Add rice; reduce heat to low. Cook, stirring constantly, 3 minutes.
3. Add broth, tomatoes, thyme, black and ground red peppers and cooked chicken mixture to rice mixture; bring liquid to a boil. Reduce heat to low; simmer, covered, stirring occasionally, 10 minutes, until about half of the liquid is absorbed.
4. Stir shrimp into rice mixture; simmer, covered, 3–5 minutes, until shrimp turn pink and all liquid is absorbed. Divide evenly among 4 plates, sprinkle with parsley and serve.

Serving ($1^1/_2$ cups) provides: $^1/_2$ Fat, $1^1/_4$ Vegetables, 2 Proteins, $1^1/_2$ Breads, 10 Optional Calories.

Per serving: 350 Calories, 10 g Total Fat, 3 g Saturated Fat, 95 mg Cholesterol, 377 mg Sodium, 42 g Total Carbohydrate, 2 g Dietary Fiber, 22 g Protein, 93 mg Calcium.

*Andouille sausage is a garlicky sausage available in gourmet food stores and some supermarkets. If you prefer, substitute the milder linguiça sausage.

CURRIED CHICKEN AND CHICK-PEA SALAD

Makes 4 servings

The flavors in this Mideastern salad are classic. Enjoy this refreshing combination for lunch, or try it on a warm evening with Indian bread for a filling supper.

1 tablespoon mild or hot curry
   powder
$^1/_2$ cup plain nonfat yogurt
2 tablespoons fresh lemon juice
1 tablespoon red wine vinegar
2 teaspoons vegetable oil
$^1/_2$ teaspoon salt
8 ounces skinless boneless cooked
   chicken breast, diced
8 ounces drained cooked chick-
   peas (garbanzo beans)

1 medium carrot, diced
1 medium tomato, diced
1 medium red onion, diced
$^1/_4$ cup golden raisins
2 tablespoons minced fresh
   cilantro
$^1/_2$ medium jalapeño pepper,
   seeded, deveined and minced,
   or to taste (wear gloves to
   prevent irritation)

1. In small nonstick skillet, toast curry powder over low heat, stirring constantly, 1 minute, until fragrant. Remove from heat; transfer curry powder to medium bowl.
2. Add yogurt, juice, vinegar, oil and salt to curry powder; stir to combine.
3. Add chicken, chick-peas, carrot, tomato, onion, raisins, cilantro and pepper to yogurt mixture; toss to combine. Refrigerate, covered, at least 2 hours. Divide evenly among 4 plates and serve.

Serving ($1^1/_4$ cups) provides: $^1/_2$ Fat, $^1/_2$ Fruit, $1^1/_2$ Vegetables, 3 Proteins, 15 Optional Calories.

Per serving: 286 Calories, 6 g Total Fat, 1 g Saturated Fat, 49 mg Cholesterol, 358 mg Sodium, 33 g Total Carbohydrate, 5 g Dietary Fiber, 26 g Protein, 123 mg Calcium.

CHICKEN, FIG AND WALNUT SALAD

Makes 4 servings

This dish is similar to Waldorf salad, but you'll find some surprise ingredients to make it even more fun to eat. Its sweet-tart flavor and crunchy-crispy-soft textures will, no doubt, make this salad a favorite.

$^1/_2$ teaspoon grated lemon zest*
2 tablespoons fresh lemon juice
1 tablespoon + 1 teaspoon
 reduced-calorie mayonnaise
1 tablespoon minced fresh dill
$^1/_2$ teaspoon salt
$^1/_4$ teaspoon freshly ground black
 pepper
8 ounces skinless boneless cooked
 chicken breast, diced

2 cups chopped Romaine lettuce
4 medium celery stalks, diced
1 small Granny Smith apple,
 cored and diced
2 dried large figs, diced
2 ounces shelled walnuts, coarsely
 chopped
2 tablespoons raisins

1. To prepare dressing, in large bowl, combine zest, juice, mayonnaise, dill, salt and pepper.
2. Add chicken, lettuce, celery, apple, figs, walnuts and raisins to dressing; toss to combine. Divide evenly among 4 plates and serve at once.

Serving (1 cup) provides: $1^1/_2$ Fats, 1 Fruit, $1^1/_2$ Vegetables, $2^1/_2$ Proteins.

Per serving: 266 Calories, 12 g Total Fat, 2 g Saturated Fat, 50 mg Cholesterol, 374 mg Sodium, 20 g Total Carbohydrate, 3 g Dietary Fiber, 21 g Protein, 70 mg Calcium.

 * *The zest of the lemon is the peel without any of the pith (white membrane). To remove zest from lemon, use a zester or the fine side of a vegetable grater.*

TURKEY-BARLEY SOUP

Makes 4 servings

This is a real old-fashioned, home-style soup, updated with the addition of Portobello mushrooms; they make the flavor richer than regular mushrooms.

2 teaspoons vegetable oil	3 ounces pearl barley
4 medium celery stalks, sliced	2 teaspoons minced fresh thyme
2 medium carrots, sliced	1 bay leaf
1 1/2 medium onions, diced	1/2 teaspoon salt
2 cups diced Portobello mushrooms	2 tablespoons minced fresh flat-leaf parsley
1 pound turkey legs or thighs, skinned*	

1. In large pot or Dutch oven, heat oil; add celery, carrots and onions. Cook over medium heat, stirring frequently, 3–5 minutes, until onions are softened. Add mushrooms; cook, stirring frequently, 5 minutes, until mushrooms release their liquid.
2. Add turkey, barley, thyme, bay leaf, salt and 4 cups water; bring liquid to a boil. Reduce heat to low; simmer, covered, 1 hour, until barley is tender and turkey is cooked through.
3. With slotted spoon, remove turkey from pot; let stand until cool enough to handle. Remove and discard bones; shred turkey.
4. Return turkey to pot; simmer, uncovered, until turkey is heated through. Remove and discard bay leaf; stir in parsley. Divide evenly among 4 bowls and serve.

Serving (1 1/2 cups) provides: 1/2 Fat, 3 Vegetables, 2 Proteins, 1 Bread.

Per serving: 236 Calories, 5 g Total Fat, 1 g Saturated Fat, 71 mg Cholesterol, 383 mg Sodium, 27 g Total Carbohydrate, 7 g Dietary Fiber, 22 g Protein, 59 mg Calcium.

One pound turkey legs or thighs will yield about 8 ounces skinned and boned cooked turkey.

TURKEY THIGH FRICASSEE

Makes 4 servings

1 teaspoon vegetable oil
Two 12-ounce turkey thighs,
   skinned and halved*
2 large Portobello mushroom
   caps, coarsely chopped
2 medium onions, minced
1 medium celery stalk, minced
$^1/_2$ medium carrot, minced
2 garlic cloves, minced
1 cup low-sodium chicken broth
1 cup low-sodium beef broth
1 bay leaf

$^1/_2$ teaspoon dried rosemary
   leaves, crumbled
$^1/_2$ teaspoon dried thyme leaves
$^1/_2$ teaspoon salt
$^1/_4$ teaspoon freshly ground black
   pepper
2 fluid ounces ($^1/_4$ cup) dry
   Marsala wine
1 tablespoon cornstarch
2 tablespoons minced fresh
   flat-leaf parsley, to garnish

1. In large nonstick skillet, heat oil; add turkey. Cook over medium-high heat, turning as needed, until browned on all sides. Reduce heat to medium-low; add mushrooms, onions, celery and carrot. Cook, stirring frequently, 10–12 minutes, until onion is golden brown. Add garlic; cook, stirring frequently, 2 minutes.
2. Add chicken and beef broths, bay leaf, rosemary, thyme, salt and pepper to turkey mixture; bring liquid to a boil. Reduce heat to low; simmer, covered, stirring occasionally, 45 minutes, until turkey is very tender.
3. Meanwhile, in small bowl, combine wine and cornstarch, stirring until cornstarch is dissolved.
4. Stir cornstarch mixture into turkey mixture; continuing to stir, cook 3 minutes, until liquid is slightly thickened. Remove and discard bay leaf. Divide evenly among 4 plates, sprinkle with parsley and serve.

Serving (3 ounces turkey with one-fourth of vegetables and sauce) provides: $^1/_4$ Fat, $1^1/_2$ Vegetables, 3 Proteins, 35 Optional Calories.

Per serving: 241 Calories, 8 g Total Fat, 2 g Saturated Fat, 75 mg Cholesterol, 406 mg Sodium, 11 g Total Carbohydrate, 2 g Dietary Fiber, 28 g Protein, 66 mg Calcium.

* Two 12-ounce turkey thighs will yield about 12 ounces skinned and boned cooked turkey.

Turkey-Bean Enchiladas

Makes 4 servings

These enchiladas are rich and satisfying; just add cooked yellow rice and a tossed salad, or sauteed spinach. Chipotle peppers are *hot*, so use them sparingly.

1 cup tomato sauce (no salt added)

$^1/_2$ cup low-sodium chicken broth

1 teaspoon pureed canned *chipotles en adobo,** or to taste

1 teaspoon vegetable oil

10 ounces skinless boneless turkey breast, cut into $^1/_4$" strips

1 medium onion, thinly sliced

1 garlic clove, minced

4 ounces drained cooked black beans, lightly mashed

3 tablespoons minced fresh cilantro

$^1/_2$ teaspoon dried oregano

$^1/_2$ teaspoon salt

$^1/_4$ teaspoon freshly ground black pepper

Eight 6" corn tortillas

$^1/_2$ cup nonfat sour cream

$1^1/_2$ ounces Monterey Jack cheese, grated

4 medium scallions, sliced, to garnish

1. Preheat oven to 350° F. Spray shallow 2-quart casserole with nonstick cooking spray.
2. In shallow bowl, combine tomato sauce, broth and *chipotles*; set aside.
3. In medium nonstick skillet, heat oil; add turkey. Cook over medium heat, stirring frequently, 5–6 minutes, until turkey is cooked through and browned on all sides. Remove turkey from skillet; set aside.
4. In same skillet, combine onion and garlic; cook over medium heat, stirring frequently, 6–7 minutes, until onion is lightly browned. Remove from heat; stir in beans, 2 tablespoons of the cilantro, the oregano, salt, black pepper and cooked turkey. Set aside.
5. To assemble enchiladas, in small nonstick skillet, heat 1 tortilla until pliable. Dip warm tortilla into tomato sauce mixture, turning to coat both sides. Spoon one-eighth of the turkey mixture along center of tortilla; fold sides of tortilla over filling to enclose. Place enchilada, seam-side down, into prepared casserole; repeat, making 7 more enchiladas.

*Chipotles en adobo—*smoked dried jalapeño peppers in a spicy tomato sauce—*are available in Latino grocery stores and some supermarkets.*

6. Spoon remaining tomato sauce mixture evenly over enchiladas. Spread with sour cream; sprinkle with cheese. Bake 20–25 minutes, until enchiladas are heated through and sauce is bubbling. Divide evenly among 4 plates, sprinkle with scallions and 1 tablespoon cilantro and serve.

Serving (2 enchiladas with one-fourth of sauce) provides: $^1/_4$ Fat, $1^1/_2$ Vegetables, 3 Proteins, 2 Breads, 25 Optional Calories.

Per serving: 337 Calories, 7 g Total Fat, 2 g Saturated Fat, 55 mg Cholesterol, 505 mg Sodium, 40 g Total Carbohydrate, 5 g Dietary Fiber, 29 g Protein, 239 mg Calcium.

Harvest Pie

Makes 4 servings

Serve this savory pie with steamed spinach or another dark green vegetable for color and flavor contrast. Have leftover cooked turkey from your holiday dinner? Simply cut 4 ounces of the cooked breast meat into chunks and add it to the sausage mixture before stirring in the dissolved cornstarch.

1 pound 8 ounces sweet potatoes, pared and cut into 1" chunks
1 teaspoon vegetable oil
5 ounces skinless boneless turkey breast, cut into 1" chunks
5 ounces lean turkey sausage, cut into 1" chunks
3 medium onions, sliced
2 medium celery stalks, diced
2 small Granny Smith apples, pared, cored and cut into $^1/_4$" slices
$1^1/_4$ cups low-sodium chicken broth

$^3/_4$ cup apple cider
1 tablespoon + 2 teaspoons cider vinegar
$^1/_2$ teaspoon dried sage leaves, crumbled
$^1/_4$ teaspoon dried thyme leaves
$^1/_2$ teaspoon salt
$^1/_4$ teaspoon freshly ground black pepper
2 teaspoons cornstarch, dissolved in 1 tablespoon cold water

1. Place sweet potatoes into medium saucepan; add water to cover. Bring liquid to a boil; reduce heat to low. Simmer 25 minutes, until potatoes are very tender.
2. Meanwhile, in large nonstick skillet, heat oil; add turkey and sausage. Cook over medium-high heat, stirring frequently, 5–8 minutes, until golden brown. With slotted spoon, remove turkey mixture from skillet; set aside.
3. In same skillet, cook onions over medium heat, stirring frequently, 8–10 minutes, until golden brown. Stir in celery and apples; cook, stirring frequently, 2 minutes.
4. Add broth, $^1/_2$ cup of the cider, 1 tablespoon of the vinegar, the sage and thyme to onion mixture; bring liquid to a boil. Reduce heat to low; simmer, covered, 15 minutes, until celery is tender.
5. Meanwhile, drain sweet potatoes, discarding liquid; return to saucepan or transfer to large bowl. With potato masher or fork, mash potatoes until as smooth as possible. Add salt, pepper, remaining $^1/_4$ cup cider and remaining 2 teaspoons vinegar; continue to mash until mixture is smooth and well combined. Set aside.

6. Preheat oven to 425° F. Spray 1¹/₂-quart baking dish with nonstick cooking spray.

7. Stir turkey mixture into onion mixture; cook until heated through. Stir in dissolved cornstarch; continuing to stir, cook until mixture is slightly thickened.

8. Transfer turkey mixture to prepared baking dish; carefully spread with sweet potato mixture. Bake 20–25 minutes, until topping is lightly browned and turkey mixture is bubbling. Divide evenly among 4 plates and serve.

Serving (one-fourth of pie) provides: ¹/₄ Fat, ³/₄ Fruit, 1 Vegetable, 2 Proteins, 1¹/₂ Breads, 20 Optional Calories.

Per serving: 329 Calories, 7 g Total Fat, 2 g Saturated Fat, 41 mg Cholesterol, 591 mg Sodium, 51 g Total Carbohydrate, 6 g Dietary Fiber, 19 g Protein, 74 mg Calcium.

TURKEY MEATLOAF

Makes 8 servings

This version of the ever-popular dish has all the flavor of the meatloaf you remember, but so much less fat!

Four 1-ounce slices whole-wheat bread, torn into pieces
2 teaspoons olive oil
4 medium celery stalks, diced
2 medium onions, chopped
1 medium carrot, chopped
1 garlic clove, minced
1 teaspoon dried marjoram
$^{1}/_{2}$ teaspoon salt
$^{1}/_{4}$ teaspoon freshly ground black pepper

1 cup canned whole Italian tomatoes (no salt added), chopped (reserve juice)
1 tablespoon firmly packed light or dark brown sugar
1 egg, beaten
$^{1}/_{2}$ medium jalapeño pepper, seeded, deveined and minced, or to taste (wear gloves to prevent irritation)
2 pounds 2 ounces ground skinless turkey breast

1. Preheat oven to 375° F. Spray 8 × 4" loaf pan with nonstick cooking spray.
2. Place bread into food processor; process until finely crumbled. Set aside.
3. In large nonstick skillet, heat oil; add celery, onions, carrot, garlic, marjoram, salt and black pepper. Cook over medium heat, stirring frequently, 3–5 minutes, until onions are softened. Remove from heat; set aside.
4. In large bowl, combine tomatoes with juice and brown sugar, stirring until sugar is dissolved. Set aside $^{1}/_{4}$ cup tomato mixture. To remaining tomato mixture, add egg, jalapeño pepper and bread crumbs; stir to combine. Add turkey; mix well. Add reserved vegetable mixture; mix until combined.
5. Pack turkey mixture lightly into prepared loaf pan; spread with reserved tomato mixture. Bake 1–1$^{1}/_{4}$ hours, until meatloaf is firm and cooked through. Remove from oven; let stand 5 minutes. Cut into 8 equal slices and serve.

Serving (one-eighth of loaf) provides: $^{1}/_{4}$ Fat, 1 Vegetable, 3$^{1}/_{2}$ Proteins, $^{1}/_{2}$ Bread, 5 Optional Calories.

Per serving: 213 Calories, 4 g Total Fat, 1 g Saturated Fat, 96 mg Cholesterol, 362 mg Sodium, 13 g Total Carbohydrate, 2 g Dietary Fiber, 32 g Protein, 40 mg Calcium.

WHITE CHILI

Makes 4 servings

This easy chili uses ground turkey breast instead of beef, chicken broth instead of tomatoes and white beans instead of kidney beans to get its "white" color. Have no fear, though—it's still pleasantly filling and wonderfully flavorful.

2 teaspoons vegetable oil
2 medium onions, chopped
2 medium celery stalks, chopped
$^1/_2$ medium carrot, chopped
2 tablespoons mild or hot chili powder
4 garlic cloves, minced
10 ounces ground skinless turkey breast
2 cups low-sodium chicken broth

4 ounces drained cooked white beans
1 tablespoon minced fresh cilantro
$^1/_4$ teaspoon cinnamon
$^1/_2$ teaspoon dried oregano
$^1/_4$ teaspoon ground red pepper
1 tablespoon + $1^1/_2$ teaspoons all-purpose flour

1. In large nonstick saucepan, heat oil; add onions, celery and carrot. Cook over medium heat, stirring frequently, 6–7 minutes, until onions are lightly browned. Add chili powder and garlic; cook, stirring frequently, 2 minutes.
2. Add turkey to vegetable mixture; cook, stirring to break up meat, 4–5 minutes, until no longer pink. Add broth, beans, cilantro, cinnamon, oregano and pepper; bring liquid to a boil. Reduce heat to low; simmer, covered, 20 minutes, until vegetables are tender and flavors are blended.
3. In small bowl, combine flour and $^1/_4$ cup water, stirring until flour is dissolved. With wire whisk, blend flour mixture into turkey mixture; simmer, uncovered, stirring occasionally, 20 minutes, until mixture is slightly thickened. Divide evenly among 4 bowls and serve.

Serving (1 cup) provides: $^1/_2$ Fat, 1 Vegetable, $2^1/_2$ Proteins, 20 Optional Calories.

Per serving: 199 Calories, 5 g Total Fat, 1 g Saturated Fat, 41 mg Cholesterol, 160 mg Sodium, 19 g Total Carbohydrate, 4 g Dietary Fiber, 23 g Protein, 73 mg Calcium.

PASTITSIO

Makes 10 servings

This filling entrée is loosely based upon the traditional Greek casserole made with ground beef or lamb. You'll probably find lots of wonderful uses for its flavorful white sauce; try it over green vegetables, potatoes, or whatever your imagination can cook up!

6 $^3/_4$ ounces ziti	$^3/_4$ ounce bulgur wheat
1 teaspoon vegetable oil	1 teaspoon salt
1 medium onion, diced	$^3/_4$ teaspoon ground nutmeg
1 pound 4 ounces ground skinless turkey breast	$^3/_4$ teaspoon ground allspice
	$^1/_2$ teaspoon cinnamon
1 $^1/_2$ cups low-sodium chicken broth	1 $^1/_2$ cups nonfat cottage cheese
	1 cup evaporated skimmed milk
$^3/_4$ cup tomato paste (no salt added)	1 tablespoon all-purpose flour
	3 ounces Parmesan cheese, grated

1. Preheat oven to 350° F. Spray 13 × 9" baking pan with nonstick cooking spray.
2. In large pot of boiling water, cook ziti 10–12 minutes, until tender. Drain, discarding liquid; set ziti aside.
3. Meanwhile, to prepare meat sauce, in large nonstick skillet, heat oil; add onion. Cook over medium heat, stirring frequently, 3–5 minutes, until onion is softened. Add turkey; cook, stirring to break up meat, 4–5 minutes, until no longer pink. Add $^3/_4$ cup of the broth, the tomato paste, bulgur, salt, nutmeg, allspice, cinnamon and $^1/_2$ cup water; bring liquid to a boil. Reduce heat to low; simmer, stirring occasionally, 20 minutes, until mixture is thickened. Remove from heat; set aside.
4. To prepare white sauce, in blender or food processor, purée cottage cheese until smooth; set aside.
5. In medium saucepan, combine milk and $^1/_2$ cup of the remaining broth; cook over medium heat until scalded.
6. Meanwhile, in small bowl, combine flour and remaining $^1/_4$ cup broth; stir until flour is dissolved.
7. Stir flour mixture into milk mixture; continuing to stir, cook 2 minutes, until mixture is smooth and thickened. Remove from heat; with wire whisk, blend in all but 1 tablespoon of the Parmesan cheese and the pureed cottage cheese, blending until mixture is combined.

8. To assemble, place half of the cooked ziti into prepared baking pan; top evenly with one third of the white sauce. Spread white sauce with meat sauce; top meat sauce with half of the remaining white sauce. Top white sauce evenly with remaining cooked ziti; top ziti with remaining white sauce. Sprinkle evenly with remaining 1 tablespoon Parmesan cheese; bake 50 minutes, until mixture is golden brown. Divide evenly among 10 plates and serve.

Serving (1 cup) provides: $^3/_4$ Vegetable, $2^1/_4$ Proteins, 1 Bread, 30 Optional Calories.

Per serving: 257 Calories, 4 g Total Fat, 2 g Saturated Fat, 43 mg Cholesterol, 595 mg Sodium, 27 g Total Carbohydrate, 2 g Dietary Fiber, 27 g Protein, 229 mg Calcium.

LENTIL–SMOKED TURKEY SOUP

Makes 4 servings

Traditionally made with ham hocks, our version of lentil soup uses smoked turkey, which provides all the wonderful flavor with lots less fat.

2 teaspoons olive oil
4 medium celery stalks, finely
   chopped
2 medium onions, chopped
1 medium carrot, chopped
2 garlic cloves, minced
6 ounces lentils, rinsed and
   drained

$^1/_4$ cup minced fresh flat-leaf
   parsley
1 bay leaf
1 teaspoon dried thyme leaves
4 cups low-sodium chicken broth
4 ounces skinless boneless
   smoked turkey breast, diced
Dash hot red pepper sauce

1. In large pot or Dutch oven, heat oil; add celery, onions and carrot. Cook over medium heat, stirring frequently, 8–10 minutes, until onions are golden brown. Add garlic; cook, stirring frequently, 2 minutes.
2. Add lentils, parsley, bay leaf and thyme to vegetable mixture; cook, stirring constantly, 1–2 minutes, until evenly coated (do not burn). Add broth and 1 cup water; bring liquid to a boil. Reduce heat to low; simmer, stirring occasionally, 30–40 minutes, until lentils are soft. Remove from heat; set aside to cool slightly. Remove and discard bay leaf.
3. Transfer lentil mixture in batches to blender or food processor; purée until smooth.
4. Return mixture to pot; add turkey. Cook over low heat, stirring frequently, until mixture is heated through. Remove from heat; just before serving, stir in pepper sauce. Divide evenly among 4 bowls and serve.

Serving (1$^1/_2$ cups) provides: $^1/_2$ Fat, 1$^1/_2$ Vegetables, 3 Proteins, 20 Optional Calories.

Per serving: 259 Calories, 6 g Total Fat, 2 g Saturated Fat, 12 mg Cholesterol, 425 mg Sodium, 35 g Total Carbohydrate, 7 g Dietary Fiber, 22 g Protein, 84 mg Calcium.

TURKEY–SWEET POTATO SALAD

Makes 4 servings

Enjoy the flavors of Thanksgiving any time of year with this festive salad. If you have leftover turkey, use it in place of the smoked turkey. Remember to zest the lemon before juicing it.

1/4 cup dried currants
3 tablespoons fresh lemon juice
1 tablespoon + 1 teaspoon vegetable oil
1 teaspoon minced fresh rosemary leaves
1 garlic clove, minced
1 pound cooked sweet potatoes, peeled and diced

7 ounces skinless boneless smoked turkey breast, cubed
1 medium red bell pepper, thinly sliced
1 medium red onion, sliced
1/4 cup minced fresh flat-leaf parsley
1 teaspoon grated lemon zest*
1 ounce sliced almonds, toasted†

1. In small bowl, combine currants and 1/4 cup hot water; let stand 10 minutes, until currants are softened. Drain currants; discard liquid.
2. To prepare dressing, in small jar with tight-fitting lid or small bowl, combine juice, oil, rosemary and garlic; cover and shake well or, with wire whisk, blend until combined.
3. To prepare salad, in large bowl, combine sweet potatoes, turkey, bell pepper, onion, parsley, zest and drained currants.
4. Pour dressing over salad; toss gently to combine. Divide evenly among 4 plates, sprinkle with almonds and serve.

Serving (1 1/2 cups) provides: 1 1/2 Fats, 1/2 Fruit, 3/4 Vegetable, 2 Proteins, 1 Bread.

Per serving: 306 Calories, 10 g Total Fat, 2 g Saturated Fat, 21 mg Cholesterol, 486 mg Sodium, 41 g Total Carbohydrate, 5 g Dietary Fiber, 14 g Protein, 70 mg Calcium.

* The zest of the lemon is the peel without any of the pith (white membrane). To remove zest from lemon, use a zester or the fine side of a vegetable grater.

† To toast almonds, in small nonstick skillet, cook almonds over low heat, stirring constantly, until golden brown; immediately transfer to heat-resistant plate to cool.

CHOUCROUTE GARNI

Makes 4 servings

Sauerkraut in plastic bags is far superior to the canned. Serve this Alsatian dish with boiled potatoes, mustard, dark bread and beer.

6 juniper berries*
1 teaspoon vegetable oil
2 medium onions, thinly sliced
1 small Granny Smith apple, pared, cored, and minced
1 large garlic clove, minced
2 cups rinsed drained sauerkraut, squeezed dry
$^1/_2$ cup dry white wine
$^1/_2$ cup low-sodium chicken broth
1 bay leaf
2 whole allspice

$^1/_2$ teaspoon dried sage leaves, crumbled
2 cups baby carrots
4 ounces smoked lean turkey sausage, cut into 4 equal pieces
One 3-ounce slice cooked boneless lean Virginia ham (about $^1/_2$" thick), cut into 4 equal strips
Freshly ground black pepper, to taste

1. Place juniper berries into small bowl; add hot water to cover. Let stand 30 minutes; drain, discarding liquid. Crush berries; set aside.
2. In large nonstick saucepan, heat oil; add onions. Cook over medium heat, stirring frequently, 3–5 minutes, until onions are softened. Add apple and garlic; cook, stirring frequently, 3 minutes, until apple is softened.
3. Add sauerkraut, wine, broth, bay leaf, allspice, sage and crushed juniper berries; bring liquid to a boil. Reduce heat to low; simmer, covered, stirring occasionally, adding 1 tablespoon water at a time if mixture begins to stick to saucepan, 30 minutes, until sauerkraut is tender and flavors are blended.
4. Add carrots, sausage and ham to sauerkraut mixture; simmer, covered, 20 minutes, until carrots are tender. Sprinkle with pepper; remove and discard bay leaf and allspice. Divide evenly among 4 plates and serve.

Serving (1$^1/_2$ cups) provides: $^1/_4$ Fat, $^1/_4$ Fruit, 2$^1/_2$ Vegetables, 1$^3/_4$ Proteins, 30 Optional Calories.

Per serving: 186 Calories, 5 g Total Fat, 1 g Saturated Fat, 29 mg Cholesterol, 943 mg Sodium, 20 g Total Carbohydrate, 3 g Dietary Fiber, 12 g Protein, 69 mg Calcium.

Juniper berries are available in the seasonings section of most gourmet food stores and some supermarkets.

LENTILS WITH SAUSAGE AND GREENS

Makes 4 servings

Here is a rich, soupy stew to cook up on a cold winter night. Serve it with chunks of crusty bread and a platter of crunchy radishes and cucumbers. Experiment with different greens—try kale, escarole, chard, mustard greens and turnip greens—to find the flavor you like best.

3 cups packed shredded well-washed trimmed assorted greens

6 ounces lentils, rinsed and drained

4 medium onions, chopped

$^1/_2$ medium carrot, chopped

4 garlic cloves, minced

4 ounces cooked sweet or hot Italian-style turkey sausage, cut into $^1/_2$" slices

10 ounces red potatoes, pared and cut into $^1/_2$" pieces

$^1/_2$ cup low-sodium chicken broth

Pinch crushed red pepper flakes, or to taste

1. In medium saucepan, bring 6 cups water to a boil; add greens. Reduce heat to medium-low; simmer, partially covered, 5 minutes, until greens are tender. Drain greens, reserving $2^1/_2$ cups liquid.
2. Return reserved liquid to same saucepan; bring to a boil. Add lentils. Reduce heat to low; simmer, covered, 10 minutes, until lentils begin to soften.
3. Meanwhile, spray medium nonstick skillet with nonstick cooking spray; heat. Add onions, carrot and garlic; cook over medium heat, stirring frequently, 3–5 minutes, until onions are softened.
4. Add sausage and cooked vegetable mixture to lentils; simmer 15 minutes.
5. Add potatoes, broth, pepper flakes and cooked greens to lentil mixture; simmer 15 minutes, until potatoes and lentils are very tender. Divide evenly among 4 bowls and serve.

Serving (1$^1/_4$ cups) provides: 2$^3/_4$ Vegetables, 3 Proteins, $^1/_2$ Bread, 5 Optional Calories.

Per serving: 325 Calories, 5 g Total Fat, 1 g Saturated Fat, 19 mg Cholesterol, 286 mg Sodium, 51 g Total Carbohydrate, 11 g Dietary Fiber, 22 g Protein, 124 mg Calcium.

FRICASSEED QUAIL

Makes 4 servings

2 teaspoons olive oil
1 teaspoon sweet butter*
Four 4-ounce quail, skinned,
    butterflied and pressed flat†
1 cup thinly sliced mushrooms
2 tablespoons minced shallot
1/2 cup low-sodium chicken broth

1/4 cup low-sodium beef broth
2 tablespoons fresh lemon juice
1/4 teaspoon freshly ground black
    pepper
2 tablespoons minced fresh
    flat-leaf parsley, to garnish

1. In large nonstick skillet, combine oil and butter; heat. Add quail, skinned-side down; cook over medium heat, turning once, 5 minutes, until browned on both sides and cooked through. Remove quail from skillet; set aside.
2. In a skillet, combine mushrooms and shallot; cook over medium heat, stirring frequently, 3–4 minutes, until mushrooms release their liquid. Continue to stir 3–4 minutes, until liquid evaporates and mushrooms are brown.
3. Add chicken and beef broths, juice and pepper to mushroom mixture; cook, scraping up browned bits from bottom of skillet, until mixture comes to a boil. Add cooked quail; cook, basting quail with pan juices, 3 minutes, until quail are heated through. With slotted spoon, transfer 1 quail to each of 4 plates; cover to keep warm.
4. Increase heat to high; cook mushroom mixture, stirring occasionally, 3–4 minutes, until liquid is reduced in volume by about half; pour evenly over warm quail. Serve sprinkled with parsley.

Serving (1 quail with 2 tablespoons mushroom mixture) provides: 1/2 Fat, 1/2 Vegetable, 2 Proteins, 15 Optional Calories.

Per serving (with butter): 151 Calories, 8 g Total Fat, 2 g Saturated Fat, 53 mg Cholesterol, 70 mg Sodium, 3 g Total Carbohydrate, 0 g Dietary Fiber, 18 g Protein, 17 mg Calcium.

Per serving (with margarine): 151 Calories, 8 g Total Fat, 2 g Saturated Fat, 50 mg Cholesterol, 70 mg Sodium, 3 g Total Carbohydrate, 0 g Dietary Fiber, 18 g Protein, 17 mg Calcium.

*One teaspoon unsalted stick margarine may be substituted for the butter. Add 1/4 Fat Selection and reduce Optional Calories to 5.

†A 4-ounce quail will yield about 2 ounces skinned and boned cooked poultry.

CORNISH HENS IN "CREAM"

Makes 4 servings

2 fluid ounces (¹/₄ cup) brandy
2 tablespoons golden raisins
2 teaspoons stick margarine
1 teaspoon vegetable oil
Two 1-pound Cornish game
   hens, skinned and halved*
¹/₂ cup low-sodium chicken broth
¹/₄ cup low-sodium beef broth

10 juniper berries†
¹/₄ teaspoon salt
¹/₄ teaspoon freshly ground black
   pepper
¹/₄ cup nonfat sour cream
2 teaspoons minced fresh tarragon or other fresh herb, or
¹/₂ teaspoon dried

1. In small bowl, combine brandy and raisins; let stand 4 hours.
2. Preheat oven to 350° F.
3. In large flameproof casserole or Dutch oven, combine margarine and oil; heat. Add hens, skinned-side down; cook over medium heat, turning as needed, 6 minutes, until hens are browned on all sides. Remove hens from casserole; set aside.
4. In same casserole, combine chicken and beef broths, juniper berries, salt, pepper and raisin mixture; bring liquid to a boil. Reduce heat to low; simmer, stirring occasionally and crushing juniper berries with back of wooden spoon, 5 minutes, until liquid is slightly reduced in volume. Remove from heat.
5. Add hens to broth mixture; baste with pan juices. Bake, covered, 30 minutes, until hens are cooked through. Transfer 1 hen half to each of 4 plates; cover to keep warm.
6. Stir sour cream and tarragon into pan juices; pour evenly over hens and serve.

Serving (1 hen half with ¹/₄ cup sour cream mixture) provides: ³/₄ Fat, ¹/₄ Fruit, 3 Proteins, 55 Optional Calories.

Per serving: 219 Calories, 7 g Total Fat, 1 g Saturated Fat, 74 mg Cholesterol, 269 mg Sodium, 5 g Total Carbohydrate, 0 g Dietary Fiber, 25 g Protein, 40 mg Calcium.

A 1-pound Cornish game hen will yield about 6 ounces skinned and boned cooked poultry.

†Juniper berries are available in the seasonings section of most gourmet food stores and some supermarkets.

6

SEAFOOD

PENNE WITH RICH TUNA SAUCE

Makes 4 servings

Tuna sauces are classics in Italy. This one is served with penne *rigate*, a ridged tubular pasta.

6 ounces penne *rigate* pasta
2 teaspoons olive oil
2 medium onions, sliced
3 garlic cloves, minced
4 medium tomatoes, diced
8 ounces drained water-packed
   chunk white tuna, flaked

2 tablespoons rinsed drained
   capers
¹/₄ cup minced fresh flat-leaf
   parsley, to garnish

1. In large pot of boiling water, cook penne 10–12 minutes, until tender. Drain, reserving ¹/₃ cup liquid; set penne and reserved liquid aside.
2. Meanwhile, in large nonstick skillet, heat oil; add onions. Cook over medium heat, stirring frequently, 3–5 minutes, until onions are softened. Add garlic; cook, stirring frequently, 2 minutes. Add tomatoes; cook, stirring frequently, 3–5 minutes, until tomatoes are softened. Stir in tuna and capers; cook, stirring frequently, 2–3 minutes, until mixture is heated through.
3. Add cooked penne and reserved liquid to tuna mixture; cook, tossing constantly, 1 minute, until pasta is heated through and well coated. Sprinkle with parsley; toss to combine. Divide evenly among 4 plates and serve.

Serving (1¹/₄ cups) provides: ¹/₂ Fat, 2¹/₂ Vegetables, 1 Protein, 2 Breads.

Per serving: 308 Calories, 5 g Total Fat, 1 g Saturated Fat, 24 mg Cholesterol, 352 mg Sodium, 44 g Total Carbohydrate, 4 g Dietary Fiber, 23 g Protein, 33 mg Calcium.

CODFISH PIE

Makes 4 servings

Here is a satisfying cold-weather supper; all it needs is some brightly colored vegetables, such as carrots and Brussels sprouts, to complete the meal. Try a baked apple for dessert.

2 cups clam juice
2 cups pearl onions
2 medium celery stalks, diced
1 medium carrot, diced
1 bay leaf
1 pound 8 ounces cod steaks
1 cup skim milk
$^3/_4$ cup evaporated skimmed milk
1 pound 9 ounces baking
   potatoes, pared and diced
$^1/_2$ teaspoon salt

Pinch ground white pepper
2 teaspoons stick margarine
1 tablespoon + 1 teaspoon
   all-purpose flour
1 teaspoon Worcestershire sauce
$^1/_4$ teaspoon dried thyme leaves
$^1/_4$ teaspoon freshly ground black
   pepper
Pinch ground red pepper
Pinch ground nutmeg
$^1/_4$ teaspoon paprika

1. Preheat oven to 400° F. Spray shallow 1-quart baking dish or four 8-ounce ramekins with nonstick cooking spray.
2. In medium nonstick skillet, bring juice to a boil; reduce heat to low. Add onions, celery, carrot and bay leaf; simmer, stirring occasionally, 10 minutes, until onions are softened.
3. Add cod to juice mixture; remove from heat. Let stand, covered, 30 minutes, until fish flakes easily when tested with fork.
4. Meanwhile, in small nonstick saucepan, combine skim and evaporated milks; cook over low heat, stirring occasionally, until scalded. Remove from heat; set aside.
5. Place potatoes into medium saucepan; add water to cover. Bring liquid to a boil; reduce heat to low. Simmer 10–15 minutes, until potatoes are tender. Drain, discarding liquid; return potatoes to saucepan. Cook over medium heat, shaking saucepan constantly, until potatoes are dry. Remove from heat.
6. With potato masher or fork, mash potatoes until as smooth as possible. With wire whisk, stir in $^1/_4$ teaspoon of the salt, the white pepper and $^1/_2$ cup + 2 tablespoons of the scalded milk mixture; set aside, covered.

7. To prepare white sauce, in medium nonstick saucepan, melt margarine; with wire whisk, stir in flour. Cook over low heat, stirring constantly with wire whisk, 2 minutes, until mixture is crumbly. Remove from heat; with wire whisk, gradually stir in 1 cup of the remaining scalded milk, blending until mixture is smooth. Add Worcestershire sauce, thyme, black and ground red peppers, nutmeg and remaining $1/4$ teaspoon salt; set aside.

8. With slotted spatula, remove cod from broth mixture. Remove and discard skin and bones from cod; cut into bite-size pieces. Place cod into prepared baking dish or divide evenly among prepared ramekins.

9. Place medium sieve over medium bowl. Strain juice mixture through sieve, reserving solids and $1^{1}/_{2}$ cups of the liquid. Remove and discard bay leaf. Arrange strained solids evenly over cod.

10. Stir strained broth into white sauce; cook over low heat, stirring constantly, until mixture comes to a simmer. Remove from heat.

11. Pour white sauce evenly over fish mixture; top with potato mixture. Brush potato mixture with remaining 2 tablespoons scalded milk; sprinkle evenly with paprika. Bake 10 minutes, until potatoes are lightly browned and mixture is heated through. Divide evenly among four plates and serve.

Serving (one-fourth of large pie or 1 ramekin) provides: $1/2$ Milk, $1/2$ Fat, $1^{3}/_{4}$ Vegetables, 2 Proteins, $1^{1}/_{4}$ Breads, 25 Optional Calories.

Per serving: 436 Calories, 4 g Total Fat, 1 g Saturated Fat, 76 mg Cholesterol, 789 mg Sodium, 58 g Total Carbohydrate, 4 g Dietary Fiber, 42 g Protein, 325 mg Calcium.

CREAMED SALMON IN TOAST BOATS

Makes 4 servings

Here is a pretty dish for a simple supper or brunch; serve it with braised cucumbers.

4 fluid ounces ($^1/_2$ cup) dry white wine
1 small onion, quartered
1 small carrot, quartered
1 small celery stalk, quartered
6 fresh flat-leaf parsley sprigs
1 bay leaf
$^1/_2$ teaspoon dried thyme leaves
$^1/_2$ teaspoon dried marjoram
$^1/_2$ teaspoon salt
$^1/_4$ teaspoon freshly ground black pepper
Pinch anise seed
1 pound 2 ounces salmon steaks
2 teaspoons stick margarine
$^1/_2$ medium onion, minced

1 tablespoon + 1 teaspoon all-purpose flour
$^1/_2$ cup thinly sliced mushroom caps
$^1/_4$ medium yellow or red bell pepper, minced
$^1/_2$ medium celery stalk, minced
$^1/_4$ cup nonfat cream cheese, softened
$^1/_2$ teaspoon dried tarragon, crumbled
$^1/_2$ teaspoon Dijon-style mustard
Four 1-ounce crusty French rolls, split and toasted
2 tablespoons minced fresh flat-leaf parsley, to garnish

1. In medium nonstick skillet, combine wine, onion, carrot and celery quarters, parsley sprigs, bay leaf, thyme, marjoram, salt, black pepper, anise seed and $1^1/_2$ cups water; bring liquid to a boil. Reduce heat to low; simmer, covered, 20 minutes, until vegetables are tender.
2. Add salmon to wine mixture; baste with liquid in skillet. Remove skillet from heat; let stand, covered, 30 minutes, until salmon flakes easily when tested with fork.
3. With slotted spatula, remove salmon from wine mixture. Set salmon aside; cover to keep warm.
4. Place medium sieve over medium bowl. Strain wine mixture through sieve, reserving liquid; discard solids. Return liquid to skillet; keep warm over low heat.

5. In medium nonstick saucepan, melt margarine; add minced onion. Cook over medium heat, stirring frequently, 3–5 minutes, until onion is softened. Add flour; cook, stirring constantly, 2 minutes, until mixture is crumbly. Remove from heat; with wire whisk, gradually stir in reserved warm liquid, blending until flour mixture is dissolved. Return saucepan to low heat; cook, stirring constantly with wire whisk, until mixture comes to a simmer and is thickened. Stir in mushrooms, bell pepper and minced celery; simmer, covered, 5 minutes, until vegetables are tender. Stir in cream cheese, tarragon and mustard; remove from heat.

6. Remove and discard skin and bones from salmon; cut salmon into bite-size pieces. Transfer salmon to cream cheese mixture; cook over low heat, stirring frequently, 1–2 minutes, just until heated through.

7. Place 2 roll halves, cut-side up, onto each of 4 plates; spoon salmon mixture evenly over rolls. Serve sprinkled with parsley.

Serving (1^1/$_4$ cups salmon mixture with 2 roll halves) provides: ^{1}/$_2$ Fat, ^{1}/$_2$ Vegetable, 3^1/$_4$ Proteins, 1 Bread, 50 Optional Calories.

Per serving: 304 Calories, 10 g Total Fat, 2 g Saturated Fat, 60 mg Cholesterol, 610 mg Sodium, 21 g Total Carbohydrate, 2 g Dietary Fiber, 26 g Protein, 99 mg Calcium.

ITALIAN STUFFED TUNA SANDWICH

Makes 4 servings

Called *Pane Bagna* in Italy, this sandwich is the perfect picnic alternative to mayonnaise-based sandwiches, and it gets even better if made in advance.

4 cups shredded lettuce
8 ounces drained water-packed
  chunk white tuna, flaked
1 medium red onion, very thinly
  sliced
1 tablespoon rinsed drained
  capers
3 tablespoons balsamic vinegar
1 tablespoon + 1 teaspoon olive
  oil

1 garlic clove, minced
1 teaspoon dried oregano
$^1/_2$ teaspoon freshly ground black
  pepper
$^1/_4$ teaspoon salt
One 8-ounce loaf Italian bread
2 medium tomatoes, sliced

1. To prepare salad, in medium bowl, combine lettuce, tuna, onion and capers; set aside.
2. To prepare dressing, in small jar with tight-fitting lid or small bowl, combine vinegar, oil, garlic, oregano, pepper and salt; cover and shake well or, with wire whisk, blend until combined.
3. Pour dressing over salad; toss to combine.
4. Split bread lengthwise almost all the way through; spread open. Line bottom half of bread with tomatoes; top evenly with salad mixture. Replace top half of bread to enclose. Wrap tightly in plastic wrap; refrigerate 2 hours, until chilled and flavors are blended. Cut loaf crosswise, through plastic wrap, into 4 equal portions.

Serving (one-fourth of loaf) provides: 1 Fat, $3^1/_4$ Vegetables, 1 Protein, 2 Breads.

Per serving: 310 Calories, 8 g Total Fat, 1 g Saturated Fat, 24 mg Cholesterol, 759 mg Sodium, 37 g Total Carbohydrate, 4 g Dietary Fiber, 21 g Protein, 102 mg Calcium.

PAELLA

Makes 4 servings

This Spanish classic has myriad versions, which isn't surprising, since it's one of the best hearty one-dish meals around.

1³/₄ cups low-sodium chicken broth
Pinch saffron threads
2 teaspoons olive oil
2 medium onions, chopped
1 medium red bell pepper, chopped
6 ounces long-grain rice
2 garlic cloves, minced
2 cups canned whole Italian tomatoes (no salt added), drained and coarsely chopped

¹/₂ cup thawed frozen green lima beans
1 teaspoon minced fresh thyme
8 ounces medium shrimp, peeled and deveined
12 medium mussels, scrubbed and debearded

1. Preheat oven to 350° F.
2. In small saucepan, bring 1 cup of the broth to a boil; remove from heat. Stir in saffron; let stand 10 minutes.
3. In paella pan or large heatproof skillet, heat oil; add onions and bell pepper. Cook over medium heat, stirring frequently, 3–5 minutes, until onions are softened. Add rice and garlic; stir until rice is well coated.
4. Add tomatoes, beans, thyme, remaining ³/₄ cup broth and reserved saffron mixture to rice mixture; bring liquid to a boil. Cook 1 minute, stirring occasionally; remove from heat.
5. Transfer pan to oven; bake 12–14 minutes, until rice is almost tender. Stir in shrimp and mussels; bake 4–5 minutes, until shrimp turn pink and mussels open (discard any mussels that do not open). Remove from oven; let stand, covered, 8 minutes. Divide evenly among 4 plates and serve.

Serving (2 cups) provides: ¹/₂ Fat, 2 Vegetables, 1¹/₄ Proteins, 1³/₄ Breads, 10 Optional Calories.

Per serving: 340 Calories, 6 g Total Fat, 1 g Saturated Fat, 94 mg Cholesterol, 427 mg Sodium, 51 g Total Carbohydrate, 4 g Dietary Fiber, 23 g Protein, 107 mg Calcium.

SEAFOOD AND MUSHROOM LASAGNA

Makes 6 servings

Lasagna is always a favorite; this version, which combines seafood and pasta in a creamy white sauce, is elegant fare. Feel free to substitute your favorite seafood for those listed below.

9 ounces curly or plain lasagna
  noodles (9 noodles)
2 tablespoons vegetable oil
2 medium onions, diced
4 cups chopped mushrooms
2 tablespoons all-purpose flour
2 cups skim milk

6 ounces cooked deveined peeled
  shrimp, chopped
6 ounces cooked monkfish fillets
6 ounces cooked crabmeat, flaked
$^1/_4$ cup minced fresh chives
Pinch ground red pepper

1. Preheat oven to 400° F.
2. In large pot of boiling water, cook lasagna noodles 10–12 minutes, until tender. Drain, discarding liquid. Place noodles into large bowl of cold water; set aside.
3. Meanwhile, in large nonstick skillet, heat 2 teaspoons of the oil; add onions. Cook over medium heat, stirring frequently, 3–5 minutes, until onions are softened. Add mushrooms; cook, stirring frequently, 5 minutes, until mushrooms release their liquid. Continuing to stir, cook until liquid is evaporated. Remove from heat; set aside.
4. To prepare white sauce, in medium nonstick saucepan, heat remaining 1 tablespoon + 1 teaspoon oil; add flour. Cook over medium-low heat, stirring constantly with wire whisk, 3 minutes, until mixture is golden brown. Remove from heat; set aside to cool.
5. Meanwhile, in small saucepan, bring $1^1/_2$ cups of the milk just to a boil; remove from heat.
6. Add remaining $^1/_2$ cup milk to cooled flour mixture, stirring with wire whisk until smooth. Continuing to stir, add flour mixture to hot milk, blending until mixture is smooth; cook over low heat, stirring constantly, 4 minutes, until mixture is slightly thickened. Remove from heat. Set aside $^1/_2$ cup of the white sauce.
7. Stir mushroom mixture into another $^1/_2$ cup of the white sauce; set aside.
8. Spread another $^1/_2$ cup of the white sauce into 13 × 9" baking pan; stir shrimp, monkfish, crabmeat, chives and pepper into remaining sauce.

9. Drain noodles. To assemble lasagna, top sauce in baking pan with 3 noodles, overlapping edges if necessary; spread with seafood mixture. Top seafood mixture with 3 more noodles; spread with mushroom mixture. Top mushroom mixture with remaining 3 noodles; spread with reserved $^1/_4$ cup sauce. Bake 30–35 minutes, until mixture is heated through and bubbling. Remove from oven; let stand 10 minutes. Divide evenly among 6 plates and serve.

Serving (one-sixth of lasagna) provides: $^1/_4$ Milk, 1 Fat, $1^3/_4$ Vegetables, $1^1/_2$ Proteins, 2 Breads, 20 Optional Calories.

Per serving: 345 Calories, 7 g Total Fat, 1 g Saturated Fat, 95 mg Cholesterol, 198 mg Sodium, 42 g Total Carbohydrate, 2 g Dietary Fiber, 27 g Protein, 162 mg Calcium.

OYSTER PO' BOY WITH RÉMOULADE SAUCE

Makes 4 servings

According to legend, this is the sandwich, *La Médiatrice* "the Peacemaker," that straying husbands would bring home to their wives. It may or may not appease anger, but it will surely soothe your hunger. For a complete meal, add a cucumber and tomato salad and a glass of beer or crisp white wine.

$^1/_4$ cup fat-free mayonnaise
1 medium scallion, minced
$^1/_4$ medium celery stalk, minced
1 tablespoon minced dill pickle
1 tablespoon minced fresh flat-
  leaf parsley
1 tablespoon red wine vinegar
2 teaspoons Dijon-style mustard
2 teaspoons rinsed drained
  capers, finely chopped
1 teaspoon Worcestershire sauce
Hot red pepper sauce, to taste
Four 1-ounce crusty French rolls,
  split and toasted

2 tablespoons all-purpose flour
$^1/_4$ teaspoon freshly ground black
  pepper
$^1/_4$ teaspoon ground red pepper
24 medium oysters, shucked
$^1/_4$ cup fat-free egg substitute
1 tablespoon vegetable oil
1 medium tomato, thinly sliced
$^1/_2$ cup shredded iceberg lettuce
1 medium lemon, cut into
  wedges

1. To prepare sauce, in small bowl, combine mayonnaise, scallion, celery, pickle, parsley, vinegar, mustard, capers, Worcestershire sauce and pepper sauce; let stand, covered, 30 minutes, until flavors are blended.
2. Meanwhile, to prepare po' boys, remove about $^1/_4$ ounce bread from each roll; set rolls aside. Crumble removed bread; transfer to sheet of wax paper or paper plate. Add flour and black and ground red peppers to crumbs; stir to combine. One at a time, dip oysters into egg substitute, then into bread crumb mixture, turning to coat evenly.
3. In large nonstick skillet, heat 1$^1/_2$ teaspoons of the oil; add half of the oysters. Cook over medium heat, turning oysters once, 1 minute, until oysters are cooked through and golden brown. Remove oysters from skillet; set aside. Repeat with remaining oil and oysters.

4. Place one-fourth of the cooked oysters, one-fourth of the tomato slices and 2 tablespoons of the lettuce in each roll. Serve with reserved sauce; garnish with lemon wedges.

Serving (1 sandwich with 1 tablespoon sauce) provides: $^3/_4$ Fat, $^3/_4$ Vegetable, $1^1/_4$ Proteins, 1 Bread, 25 Optional Calories.

Per serving: 197 Calories, 6 g Total Fat, 1 g Saturated Fat, 31 mg Cholesterol, 524 mg Sodium, 25 g Total Carbohydrate, 2 g Dietary Fiber, 9 g Protein, 66 mg Calcium.

SEAFOOD GUMBO

Makes 4 servings

For a wonderful hot meal, serve this New Orleans classic over cooked rice. Filé powder, the spice made from ground sassafras that gives gumbo its distinctive flavor, is readily available in the seasonings section of most supermarkets.

2 teaspoons vegetable oil
2 medium celery stalks, chopped
1 medium onion, chopped
$^{1}/_{2}$ medium green bell pepper, chopped
2 ounces cooked boneless lean ham, diced
2 cups okra, cut into 1" chunks
2 cups canned crushed tomatoes (no salt added)

1 bay leaf
Pinch freshly ground black pepper
Pinch ground red pepper
8 ounces shrimp, peeled and deveined
1 teaspoon filé powder

1. In large nonstick skillet, heat oil; add celery, onion, bell pepper and ham. Cook over medium heat, stirring frequently, 6–7 minutes, until onion is lightly browned.
2. Add okra, tomatoes, bay leaf, black and ground red peppers and 2 cups water; bring liquid to a boil. Reduce heat to low; simmer, covered, 12–15 minutes, until okra is tender.
3. Stir shrimp and filé powder into tomato mixture; cook, stirring frequently, 3–5 minutes, until shrimp turn pink. Remove and discard bay leaf. Divide evenly among 4 plates and serve.

Serving ($1^{1}/_{4}$ cups) provides: $^{1}/_{2}$ Fat, $2^{3}/_{4}$ Vegetables, $1^{1}/_{4}$ Proteins.

Per serving: 161 Calories, 4 g Total Fat, 1 g Saturated Fat, 94 mg Cholesterol, 288 mg Sodium, 14 g Total Carbohydrate, 3 g Dietary Fiber, 17 g Protein, 116 mg Calcium.

SEAFOOD STEW

Makes 4 servings

12 medium mussels, scrubbed and debearded, or clams, scrubbed
2 teaspoons olive oil
1 medium onion, chopped
4 fluid ounces ($^1/_2$ cup) dry white wine
2 garlic cloves, minced
2 cups canned whole Italian tomatoes, drained and chopped

$^1/_4$ cup minced fresh flat-leaf parsley
$^1/_4$ teaspoon ground red pepper
5 ounces monkfish fillets, cut into 1" chunks
5 ounces large shrimp, peeled and deveined
Eight $^1/_2$-ounce slices Italian bread, toasted

1. In large pot or Dutch oven, bring $^1/_2$ cup water to a boil; add mussels. Cook, covered, 4–5 minutes, until mussels open (discard any mussels that do not open). With slotted spoon, remove mussels from pot; set aside.
2. Line medium sieve with coffee filter or double layer of cheesecloth; place over heat-resistant bowl. Pour liquid in pot through sieve. Reserve liquid; discard solids. Wipe pot dry.
3. In same pot, heat oil; add onion. Cook over medium heat, stirring frequently, 3–5 minutes, until onion is softened. Add wine and garlic; bring liquid to a boil. Cook, stirring occasionally, 2 minutes, until liquid is slightly reduced in volume.
4. Add tomatoes, parsley, pepper and strained liquid to onion mixture; bring liquid to a boil. Reduce heat to low; simmer, stirring occasionally, 10 minutes, until mixture is slightly thickened.
5. Add fish and shrimp to tomato mixture; simmer 4–5 minutes, until fish flakes easily when tested with fork and shrimp turn pink. Add mussels; simmer 1 minute, until mussels are heated through.
6. Place 2 toast slices in each of 4 bowls; spoon one-fourth of the stew onto each portion of toast.

Serving (1 cup stew, 2 toast slices) provides: $^1/_2$ Fat, $1^1/_4$ Vegetables, $1^1/_2$ Proteins, 1 Bread, 25 Optional Calories.

Per serving: 242 Calories, 5 g Total Fat, 1 g Saturated Fat, 71 mg Cholesterol, 505 mg Sodium, 24 g Total Carbohydrate, 2 g Dietary Fiber, 20 g Protein, 97 mg Calcium.

MEATLESS

WINTER VEGETABLE SOUP

Makes 4 servings

Here is a creamy soup to serve for a soup-and-salad supper. Add some crusty bread and your meal is complete.

2 teaspoons stick margarine
3 medium onions, chopped
10 ounces baking potatoes, pared and diced
1 cup low-sodium vegetable broth
2 medium celery stalks, chopped
$^1/_2$ medium white turnip, pared and diced
$^1/_2$ medium carrot, diced

$^1/_2$ cup diced parsnip
1 bay leaf
$^1/_4$ teaspoon dried marjoram or thyme leaves
$^1/_4$ teaspoon salt
Freshly ground black pepper, to taste
$^1/_2$ cup skim milk
$^1/_2$ cup evaporated skimmed milk
$^1/_4$ cup minced fresh flat-leaf parsley

1. In large nonstick saucepan, melt margarine; add onions. Cook over medium heat, stirring frequently, 3–5 minutes, until onions are softened.
2. Add potatoes, broth, celery, turnip, carrot, parsnip, bay leaf, marjoram, salt, pepper and $^1/_2$ cup water; bring liquid to a boil. Reduce heat to low; simmer, covered, 15–20 minutes, until vegetables are tender. Remove and discard bay leaf.
3. With slotted spoon, transfer solids to food processor, blender or food mill; purée until smooth. Return vegetables to saucepan; stir in skim and evaporated milks and parsley. Cook over low heat, stirring occasionally, 5 minutes, until mixture is heated through (do not boil). Divide evenly among 4 bowls and serve.

Serving (1$^1/_4$ cups) provides: $^1/_4$ Milk, $^1/_2$ Fat, 1$^1/_2$ Vegetables, $^3/_4$ Bread, 15 Optional Calories.

Per serving: 166 Calories, 2 g Total Fat, 0 g Saturated Fat, 2 mg Cholesterol, 259 mg Sodium, 31 g Total Carbohydrate, 4 g Dietary Fiber, 6 g Protein, 176 mg Calcium.

MINESTRONE

Makes 4 servings

Vary the taste by adding different vegetables or substituting navy or great Northern beans for the pinto beans.

2 teaspoons olive oil
1 medium onion, thinly sliced
2 medium celery stalks, diced
$^1/_2$ medium carrot, diced
3 garlic cloves, minced
2 cups canned whole Italian tomatoes (no salt added), coarsely chopped (reserve juice)
2 cups low-sodium vegetable broth
2 tablespoons minced fresh basil
2 tablespoons minced fresh flat-leaf parsley

$^1/_2$ teaspoon dried thyme leaves
$^1/_2$ teaspoon dried oregano
2 medium zucchini, diced
4 ounces drained cooked pinto beans
3 ounces elbow macaroni
Pinch salt
1 tablespoon + 1 teaspoon freshly grated Parmesan cheese, to garnish
Freshly ground black pepper, to taste

1. In large nonstick saucepan, heat oil; add onion. Cook over medium heat, stirring frequently, 3–5 minutes, until onion is softened. Add celery, carrot and garlic; cook, stirring frequently, 5 minutes, until onions are golden brown.
2. Add tomatoes with juice, broth, basil, parsley, thyme, oregano and 4 cups water to vegetable mixture; bring liquid to a boil. Reduce heat to low; simmer, covered, stirring occasionally, 30 minutes, until vegetables are tender.
3. Add zucchini, beans, macaroni and salt to broth mixture; simmer, stirring occasionally, 15 minutes, until macaroni is tender. Divide evenly among 4 bowls, sprinkle evenly with cheese and pepper and serve.

Serving ($1^3/_4$ cups) provides: $^1/_2$ Fat, $2^3/_4$ Vegetables, $^1/_2$ Protein, 1 Bread, 20 Optional Calories.

Per serving: 221 Calories, 4 g Total Fat, 1 g Saturated Fat, 1 mg Cholesterol, 321 mg Sodium, 39 g Total Carbohydrate, 4 g Dietary Fiber, 8 g Protein, 123 mg Calcium.

BLACK BEAN SOUP

Makes 4 servings

Few things are more satisfying than a good black bean soup. Here's one you'll love, full of the flavor of South American cuisine. For an exciting color and temperature contrast, top each bowl of soup with a dollop of plain nonfat yogurt or nonfat sour cream.

6 ounces dry black beans, picked over, rinsed and drained
2 teaspoons olive oil
2 medium onions, chopped
1 medium red bell pepper, chopped
$^1/_2$ medium jalapeño pepper, seeded, deveined and minced, (wear gloves to prevent irritation)

2 garlic cloves, minced
1 teaspoon ground cumin
1 teaspoon dried oregano
Pinch ground cloves
4 cups low-sodium vegetable broth

1. Place beans into medium bowl; add cold water to cover. Let stand overnight.*
2. Drain beans; discard liquid. Set beans aside.
3. In large nonstick saucepan, heat oil; add onions, bell and jalapeño peppers and garlic. Cook over medium heat, stirring frequently, 3–5 minutes, until onions are softened. Add cumin, oregano and cloves; cook, stirring constantly, 2 minutes, until mixture is thoroughly combined.
4. Add broth and drained beans to onion mixture; bring liquid to a boil. Reduce heat to low; simmer, stirring occasionally, $1^1/_4$–$1^1/_2$ hours, until beans are very tender. Divide evenly among 4 bowls and serve.

Serving (1 cup) provides: $^1/_2$ Fat, $1^1/_4$ Vegetables, 2 Proteins, 20 Optional Calories.

Per serving: 137 Calories, 3 g Total Fat, 0 g Saturated Fat, 0 mg Cholesterol, 77 mg Sodium, 40 g Total Carbohydrate, 7 g Dietary Fiber, 11 g Protein, 77 mg Calcium.

* If you prefer to quick-soak the beans, combine the beans and enough cold water to cover in a large saucepan. Bring to a boil over high heat; boil 2 minutes. Remove from heat; let stand 1 hour, covered. Proceed with step 2.

AROMATIC WHITE BEAN SOUP WITH VEGETABLES

Makes 4 servings

6 ounces dry great Northern beans, picked over, rinsed and drained

2 teaspoons olive oil

2 medium fennel bulbs, chopped

2 medium onions, chopped

2 medium celery stalks, chopped

2 tablespoons grated pared fresh ginger root

2 garlic cloves, minced

1 bay leaf

$^1/_2$ teaspoon crushed red pepper flakes

8 ounces cooked all-purpose potatoes, diced

$1^1/_2$ medium tomatoes, diced

$^1/_4$ cup minced fresh flat-leaf parsley or cilantro

1 teaspoon salt

$^1/_4$–$^1/_2$ teaspoon ground white pepper

2 tablespoons fresh lemon juice

1. Place beans into medium bowl; add cold water to cover. Let stand overnight.*
2. Drain beans; discard liquid. Set beans aside.
3. In large nonstick saucepan, heat oil; add fennel, onions and celery. Cook over medium heat, stirring frequently, 3–5 minutes, until onions are softened. Add ginger and garlic; cook, stirring constantly, 1 minute, until vegetables are evenly coated (do not burn).
4. Add bay leaf, pepper flakes, drained beans and 5 cups water; bring liquid to a boil. Reduce heat to low; simmer, stirring occasionally, 45 minutes. Remove from heat; set aside to cool slightly. Remove and discard bay leaf.
5. Transfer bean mixture in batches to food processor; purée until smooth.
6. Return mixture to saucepan; add potatoes, tomatoes, parsley, salt and white pepper. Cook over low heat, stirring frequently, until mixture is heated through. Remove from heat; just before serving, stir in juice. Divide evenly among 4 bowls and serve.

Serving ($1^1/_4$ cups) provides: $^1/_2$ Fat, $2^1/_2$ Vegetables, 2 Proteins, $^1/_2$ Bread.

Per serving: 262 Calories, 3 g Total Fat, 0 g Saturated Fat, 0 mg Cholesterol, 635 mg Sodium, 49 g Total Carbohydrate, 20 g Dietary Fiber, 12 g Protein, 138 mg Calcium.

* If you prefer to quick-soak the beans, combine the beans and enough cold water to cover in a large saucepan. Bring to a boil over high heat; boil 2 minutes. Remove from heat; let stand 1 hour, covered. Proceed with step 2.

BARLEY-HERB CASSEROLE

Makes 4 servings

This lovely barley pilaf combines the sweetness of butternut squash with the delightful fragrance of fresh herbs.

1 teaspoon vegetable oil	1 medium tomato, diced
1 medium onion, chopped	4 ounces drained cooked chick-peas
1 cup diced pared butternut	(garbanzo beans)
squash	3 tablespoons minced fresh flat-leaf
3$^3/_4$ ounces pearl barley	parsley
$^1/_2$ teaspoon salt	1 teaspoon minced fresh rosemary
$^1/_2$ teaspoon freshly ground black	leaves
pepper	2 cups low-sodium vegetable broth

1. Preheat oven to 350° F.
2. In large nonstick skillet, heat oil; add onion and squash. Cook over medium heat, stirring frequently, 6–7 minutes, until onion is lightly browned. Add barley, salt and $^1/_4$ teaspoon of the pepper; cook, stirring constantly, 1 minute, until mixture is thoroughly combined. Remove from heat; stir in tomato, chick-peas, parsley, rosemary and remaining $^1/_4$ teaspoon pepper.
3. Transfer barley mixture to 1$^1/_2$-quart baking dish; add broth. Bake, covered, 1 hour; bake, uncovered, 15 minutes, until liquid is absorbed and mixture is heated through. Divide evenly among 4 plates and serve.

Serving (1 cup) provides: $^1/_4$ Fat, $^3/_4$ Vegetable, $^1/_2$ Protein, 1$^1/_2$ Breads, 10 Optional Calories.

Per serving: 196 Calories, 3 g Total Fat, 0 g Saturated Fat, 0 mg Cholesterol, 320 mg Sodium, 40 g Total Carbohydrate, 7 g Dietary Fiber, 7 g Protein, 52 mg Calcium.

Chick-Pea and Fennel Stew

Makes 6 servings

Fennel gives this robust stew a subtle anise flavor.

1 tablespoon olive oil

8 medium onions, finely chopped

2 tablespoons minced fresh flat-leaf parsley

4 garlic cloves, minced

3 medium fennel bulbs, thinly sliced

2 cups low-sodium vegetable broth

2 medium tomatoes, diced

1 medium jalapeño pepper, seeded, deveined and minced, or to taste (wear gloves to prevent irritation)

1/4 teaspoon freshly ground black pepper

1 pound 8 ounces drained cooked chick-peas (garbanzo beans)

1. In large nonstick skillet, heat oil; add onions, parsley and garlic. Cook over medium heat, stirring frequently, 8–10 minutes, until onions are golden brown. Add fennel; cook, stirring frequently, 10 minutes, until tender.
2. Add broth, tomatoes and jalapeño and black peppers to onion mixture; bring liquid to a boil. Reduce heat to low; simmer, covered, stirring occasionally, 10 minutes, until tomatoes are softened and flavors are blended.
3. Stir in chick-peas; cook, covered, 5 minutes, until mixture is heated through. Divide evenly among 4 plates and serve.

Serving (1 cup) provides: 1/2 Fat, 3 1/4 Vegetables, 2 Proteins, 5 Optional Calories.

Per serving: 285 Calories, 6 g Total Fat, 1 g Saturated Fat, 0 mg Cholesterol, 95 mg Sodium, 48 g Total Carbohydrate, 7 g Dietary Fiber, 13 g Protein, 113 mg Calcium.

MEXICAN RICE AND BEAN SALAD

Makes 4 servings

4 ounces long-grain rice
$^1/_2$ teaspoon turmeric
1 teaspoon salt
8 ounces drained cooked black beans
2 cups shredded Romaine or iceberg lettuce
1 medium tomato, diced
1 medium white onion, chopped
4 ounces diced pared avocado
$^1/_2$ medium jalapeño pepper, seeded, deveined and minced, (wear gloves to prevent irritation)

$^1/_2$ cup cooked corn kernels
1 tablespoon slivered fresh cilantro
$1^1/_2$ teaspoons ground cumin
2 tablespoons fresh lime juice
1 tablespoon + 1 teaspoon vegetable oil
1 teaspoon distilled white vinegar
$^1/_4$ teaspoon freshly ground black pepper
Hot red pepper sauce, to taste

1. To prepare salad, in medium saucepan, bring $1^1/_4$ cups water to a boil; add rice, turmeric and $^1/_2$ teaspoon of the salt. Reduce heat to low; simmer, covered, 20 minutes, until rice is tender and all liquid is absorbed. Remove from heat; set aside to cool slightly.
2. In large bowl, combine beans, lettuce, tomato, onion, avocado, jalapeño pepper, corn, cilantro and cooled rice; set aside.
3. To prepare dressing, in small nonstick skillet, toast cumin over low heat, stirring constantly, 1 minute, until fragrant. Remove from heat; transfer cumin to small jar with tight-fitting lid or small bowl. Add juice, oil, vinegar, black pepper, pepper sauce and remaining $^1/_2$ teaspoon salt; cover and shake well or, with wire whisk, blend until combined.
4. Pour dressing over salad; toss gently to combine. Divide evenly among 4 plates and serve.

Serving ($1^1/_2$ cups) provides: 2 Fats, 2 Vegetables, 1 Protein, $1^1/_4$ Breads.

Per serving: 314 Calories, 10 g Total Fat, 1 g Saturated Fat, 0 mg Cholesterol, 568 mg Sodium, 49 g Total Carbohydrate, 4 g Dietary Fiber, 10 g Protein, 57 mg Calcium.

RICE PANCAKES WITH CHARD AND BEANS

Makes 4 servings

This intriguing vegetarian entrée is hearty enough to satisfy a big appetite. It's so easy to prepare you'll want to make it often.

2 teaspoons olive oil
1 medium onion, chopped
4 cups chopped well-washed
   trimmed Swiss chard
2 garlic cloves, minced
$1/4$ teaspoon salt
$1/4$ teaspoon freshly ground black
   pepper
1 cup canned whole Italian
   tomatoes (no salt added),
   chopped (reserve juice)

4 ounces drained cooked
   cannellini (white kidney) beans
2 cups cooked long-grain rice
2 egg whites
$1^1/2$ ounces Parmesan cheese,
   grated
2 tablespoons minced fresh basil

1. Line baking sheet with foil; spray with nonstick baking spray. Preheat broiler.
2. In large nonstick skillet, heat oil; add onion. Cook over medium heat, stirring frequently, 3–5 minutes, until onion is softened. Add chard, garlic, salt and pepper; cook, stirring frequently, 3 minutes, until chard is wilted. Add tomatoes with juice and beans; bring liquid to a boil. Reduce heat to low; simmer, covered, 10 minutes, until slightly thickened.
3. Meanwhile, in medium bowl, combine rice, egg whites, cheese and basil. Divide into four equal mounds and place on prepared baking sheet, leaving about 2" between each mound; with back of spoon, flatten into 5" circles. Broil 4" from heat 4–5 minutes, until just firm and lightly browned.
4. With spatula, transfer each pancake to plate; top each with one-fourth of the chard mixture.

Serving (1 pancake with $3/4$ cup chard mixture) provides: $1/2$ Fat, $2^3/4$ Vegetables, 1 Protein, 1 Bread, 10 Optional Calories.

Per serving: 278 Calories, 6 g Total Fat, 2 g Saturated Fat, 8 mg Cholesterol, 539 mg Sodium, 42 g Total Carbohydrate, 2 g Dietary Fiber, 13 g Protein, 221 mg Calcium.

BROWN RICE AND VEGETABLE SAUTÉ

Makes 4 servings

In this vegetarian entrée, reminiscent of dishes served in Morocco, the nutty flavor of brown rice and the vibrant colors of fresh vegetables meld with fragrant cumin and garlic.

2 teaspoons olive oil
4 medium carrots, diced
1 medium onion, chopped
1 medium green or red
   bell pepper, diced
1 garlic clove, minced
1 teaspoon ground cumin
2 cups cooked brown rice

4 ounces drained cooked chick-peas
   (garbanzo beans)
$1/2$ cup orange juice
$1/2$ teaspoon cinnamon
$1/4$ teaspoon salt
$1/4$ cup minced fresh flat-leaf parsley
1 tablespoon fresh lemon juice
1 ounce slivered almonds, toasted*

1. In large nonstick skillet, heat oil; add carrots, onion and bell pepper. Cook over medium heat, stirring frequently, 3–5 minutes, until onion is softened. Add garlic and cumin; cook, stirring frequently, 2 minutes.
2. Stir rice, chick-peas, orange juice, cinnamon and salt into vegetable mixture; cook, covered, 10 minutes, until vegetables are tender. Remove from heat.
3. Stir parsley and lemon juice into rice mixture. Divide evenly among 4 plates, sprinkle with almonds and serve.

Serving (1 cup) provides: 1 Fat, $1/4$ Fruit, $2^3/4$ Vegetables, $3/4$ Protein, 1 Bread.

Per serving: 294 Calories, 8 g Total Fat, 1 g Saturated Fat, 0 mg Cholesterol, 182 mg Sodium, 50 g Total Carbohydrate, 8 g Dietary Fiber, 8 g Protein, 94 mg Calcium.

   * *To toast almonds, in small nonstick skillet, cook almonds over low heat, stirring constantly, until golden brown; immediately transfer to heat-resistant plate to cool.*

WILD RICE AND CRANBERRY-STUFFED ACORN SQUASH

Makes 4 servings

3 cups low-sodium vegetable broth
8 ounces wild rice
¼ cup dried cranberries
1 tablespoon grated lemon zest*

2 teaspoons unsalted butter†
Two 1-pound acorn squash, halved and seeded‡
1 tablespoon + 1 teaspoon maple syrup

1. Preheat oven to 400° F.
2. In medium saucepan, bring broth to a boil; stir in rice, cranberries and zest. Return liquid to a boil. Reduce heat to low; simmer, covered, 45 minutes, until rice is tender. Remove from heat; let stand until all liquid is absorbed.
3. Meanwhile, spoon ½ teaspoon of the butter into seed cavity of each squash half. Place squash onto baking sheet, cut-side up; bake 40 minutes, until squash is golden brown and tender.
4. Fill seed cavity of each squash half with one fourth of the rice mixture; drizzle 1 teaspoon of the syrup over each portion of rice, and serve.

Serving (1 stuffed squash half) provides: ½ Fruit, 3 Breads, 50 Optional Calories.

Per serving (with butter): 354 Calories, 3 g Total Fat, 1 g Saturated Fat, 5 mg Cholesterol, 64 mg Sodium, 70 g Total Carbohydrate, 9 g Dietary Fiber, 10 g Protein, 75 mg Calcium.

Per serving (with margarine): 354 Calories, 3 g Total Fat, 0 g Saturated Fat, 0 mg Cholesterol, 64 mg Sodium, 71 g Total Carbohydrate, 9 g Dietary Fiber, 10 g Protein, 75 mg Calcium.

*The zest of the lemon is the peel without any of the pith (white membrane). To remove zest from lemon, use a zester or the fine side of a vegetable grater; wrap lemon in plastic wrap and refrigerate for use at another time.

† Two teaspoons unsalted stick margarine may be substituted for the butter. Add ½ Fat Selection and reduce Optional Calories to 30.

‡A 1-pound acorn squash, when halved and seeded, will weigh about 14 ounces.

BUTTERNUT SQUASH CHILI

Makes 4 servings

Squash is an important part of Mexican cuisine. This recipe uses butternut squash and other traditional ingredients and flavorings to create a meatless chili you'll love!

2 teaspoons vegetable oil
3 medium onions, diced
2 cups diced pared butternut squash
1 garlic clove, minced
2 teaspoons mild or hot chili powder
1 teaspoon ground cumin
$^1/_2$ teaspoon cinnamon

$^1/_4$ teaspoon ground cloves
2 cups canned whole Italian tomatoes (no salt added), chopped (reserve juice)
4 ounces drained cooked black beans
2 tablespoons dried currants
$^1/_2$ teaspoon salt

1. In large nonstick skillet, heat oil; add onions. Cook over medium heat, stirring frequently, 3–5 minutes, until onions are softened. Add squash and garlic; cook, stirring frequently, 5 minutes, until onions are golden brown.
2. Add chili powder, cumin, cinnamon and cloves to onion mixture; cook, stirring constantly, 1 minute, until onion mixture is evenly coated (do not burn). Stir in tomatoes with juice, beans, currants and salt; bring mixture to a boil. Reduce heat to low; simmer, stirring occasionally, 25 minutes, until squash is tender. Divide evenly among 4 bowls and serve.

Serving (1 cup) provides: $^1/_2$ Fat, $^1/_4$ Fruit, $1^3/_4$ Vegetables, $^1/_2$ Protein, $^1/_2$ Bread.

Per serving: 158 Calories, 3 g Total Fat, 0 g Saturated Fat, 0 mg Cholesterol, 488 mg Sodium, 30 g Total Carbohydrate, 4 g Dietary Fiber, 6 g Protein, 105 mg Calcium.

MIXED BEAN CHILAQUILES

Makes 4 servings

In this simple dish with a south-of-the-border flair, the wonderful flavors of vegetables, beans and cheese mingle with tender tortillas that melt in your mouth.

Four 6" corn tortillas, cut into
  $^1/_4$–$^1/_2$" strips
2 teaspoons vegetable oil
1 medium onion, chopped
1 medium red or green bell
  pepper, finely chopped
1 medium jalapeño pepper,
  seeded, deveined and minced,
  or to taste (wear gloves to
  prevent irritation)
1 garlic clove, minced

2 cups canned whole Italian
  tomatoes (no salt added),
  chopped (reserve juice)
2 tablespoons minced fresh cilantro
4 ounces drained cooked black
  beans
4 ounces drained cooked pinto
  beans
3 ounces Monterey Jack cheese,
  grated

1. Preheat oven to 350° F. Spray 9" square baking pan with nonstick cooking spray.
2. Arrange tortilla strips on nonstick baking sheet; bake, turning strips frequently, 8 minutes, until golden and crisp. Remove tortillas from oven; leave oven on. Set tortillas aside.
3. In large nonstick skillet, heat oil; add onion and bell and jalapeño peppers. Cook over medium heat, stirring frequently, 3–5 minutes, until onion is softened. Add garlic; cook, stirring frequently, 2 minutes. Add tomatoes with juice; cook, stirring frequently, 8 minutes, until mixture is slightly thickened. Stir in cilantro; remove from heat.
4. Arrange baked tortilla strips evenly in prepared baking pan; top evenly with black and pinto beans and tomato mixture. Sprinkle evenly with cheese; bake 20 minutes, until mixture is bubbling. Divide evenly among 4 plates and serve.

Serving (one-fourth of mixture) provides: $^1/_2$ Fat, 2 Vegetables, 2 Proteins, 1 Bread.

Per serving: 274 Calories, 10 g Total Fat, 4 g Saturated Fat, 22 mg Cholesterol, 352 mg Sodium, 35 g Total Carbohydrate, 5 g Dietary Fiber, 13 g Protein, 264 mg Calcium.

RICE AND BEAN BURRITOS

Makes 4 servings

1 cup canned crushed tomatoes
  (no salt added)
1 teaspoon chili powder
$^1/_2$ teaspoon ground cumin
$^1/_2$ teaspoon salt
2 teaspoons vegetable oil
2 medium onions, diced
1 medium red bell pepper, diced
1 medium green bell pepper, diced

2 garlic cloves, minced
6 ounces drained cooked pinto beans
1 tablespoon red wine vinegar
Pinch freshly ground black pepper
Four 6" flour tortillas
1 cup cooked brown rice
$1^1/_2$ ounces Monterey Jack cheese,
  grated

1. Preheat oven to 375° F. Line baking sheet with foil.
2. In small saucepan, combine tomatoes, chili powder, cumin, $^1/_4$ teaspoon of the salt and $^1/_2$ cup water; bring liquid to a boil. Reduce heat to low; simmer, covered, 10 minutes, until mixture is slightly thickened and flavors are blended. Remove from heat; set aside.
3. In large nonstick skillet, heat oil; add onions. Cook over medium heat, stirring frequently, 3–5 minutes, until onions are softened. Add red and green bell peppers and garlic; cook, stirring frequently, 5 minutes, until peppers are tender. Remove from heat; set aside.
4. In blender or food processor, combine beans, vinegar, black pepper, 1 tablespoon water and remaining $^1/_4$ teaspoon salt; purée until smooth. Set aside.
5. Place tortillas onto work surface. Spread one fourth of the bean mixture along center of each tortilla; top each portion of bean mixture with one fourth of the vegetable mixture, $^1/_4$ cup of the rice, one fourth of the cheese and 2 tablespoons of the tomato mixture. Roll tortillas tightly to enclose filling; place seam-side down onto prepared baking sheet. Bake 10 minutes, until heated through. Divide burritos among 4 plates; top each with one-fourth of the remaining tomato mixture.

Serving (1 burrito with 3 tablespoons tomato topping) provides: $^1/_2$ Fat, 2 Vegetables, $1^1/_4$ Proteins, $^1/_2$ Breads.

Per serving: 283 Calories, 8 g Total Fat, 3 g Saturated Fat, 11 mg Cholesterol, 446 mg Sodium, 44 g Total Carbohydrate, 5 g Dietary Fiber, 11 g Protein, 167 mg Calcium.

THE BEST BURRITOS

Makes 6 servings

These burritos are made with the traditional beans, rice and sour cream, but use your imagination and wrap a tortilla around sauteed vegetables, or even an egg-white omelet! Serve with spicy salsa for a delicious flavor and texture contrast.

$1^1/_2$ cups refried beans
2 teaspoons mild or hot chili powder
$^1/_4$ teaspoon ground cumin
$1^1/_2$ medium tomatoes, seeded and diced
1 medium onion, diced

Six 6" flour tortillas
$1^1/_2$ cups hot cooked long-grain rice
$^1/_3$ cup + 2 teaspoons nonfat sour cream
6 ounces Monterey Jack cheese, shredded
$^3/_4$ cup shredded lettuce

1. Preheat oven to 200° F.
2. In medium bowl, combine beans, chili powder and cumin; set aside.
3. Spray large nonstick skillet with nonstick cooking spray; heat. Add tomatoes and onion; cook over medium heat, stirring frequently, 3–5 minutes, until onion is softened. Stir in reserved bean mixture; cook, stirring constantly, 8–10 minutes, until vegetable are very soft. Remove from heat; keep warm.
4. In small nonstick skillet, heat 1 tortilla, turning once, 15 seconds, until warm; place onto work surface. Spoon one sixth of the bean mixture onto one side of tortilla 1" from edge; top with $^1/_4$ cup of the rice, then 1 tablespoon of the sour cream, 1 ounce of the cheese and 2 tablespoons of the lettuce. Fold the near edge of tortilla over filling; fold sides of tortilla inward, then roll up to enclose. Place each burrito, seam-side down, onto a heat-resistant plate; cover and keep warm in oven. Repeat, making 5 more burritos, and serve.

Serving (1 burrito) provides: 1 Vegetable, 2 Proteins, $1^1/_2$ Breads, 65 Optional Calories.

Per serving: 333 Calories, 11 g Total Fat, 6 g Saturated Fat, 30 mg Cholesterol, 540 mg Sodium, 42 g Total Carbohydrate, 2 g Dietary Fiber, 16 g Protein, 303 mg Calcium.

GREEK-FLAVORED VEGETARIAN PIE

Makes 4 servings

Similar to shepherd's pie but without the meat, this potato-topped vegetable pie with dill, olives and feta cheese, will become a favorite. Use seasonal vegetables to add variety and different flavoring to this dish.

2 teaspoons olive oil
16 medium scallions, chopped
4 cups chopped mushrooms
2 garlic cloves, minced
Pinch salt
Pinch freshly ground black
  pepper
3 large plum tomatoes, diced

2 cups steamed broccoli florets,
  chopped
2 tablespoons minced fresh dill
1 pound cooked potatoes, peeled
  and mashed
3 ounces feta cheese, crumbled
6 large kalamata olives, pitted and
  chopped

1. Preheat oven to 375° F. Spray 9" square baking pan with nonstick cooking spray.
2. In large nonstick skillet, heat oil; add scallions. Cook over medium heat, stirring frequently, 2–3 minutes, until scallions are softened. Add mushrooms, garlic, salt and pepper; cook, stirring frequently, 3–4 minutes, until mushrooms release their liquid. Continuing to stir, cook 3–4 minutes, until liquid is evaporated and mushrooms are golden brown. Add tomatoes; cook, stirring frequently, 3–5 minutes, until tomatoes are softened. Add broccoli and dill; stir to combine. Remove from heat; set aside.
3. In medium bowl, combine potatoes and cheese; set aside.
4. Transfer vegetable mixture to prepared baking pan. Top vegetable mixture evenly with olives; spread evenly with potato mixture. Bake 30 minutes, until potato topping is golden brown. Divide evenly among 4 plates and serve.

Serving (one-fourth of pie) provides: ³/4 Fat, 4¹/4 Vegetables, 1 Protein, 1 Bread.

Per serving: 257 Calories, 10 g Total Fat, 4 g Saturated Fat, 19 mg Cholesterol, 536 mg Sodium, 36 g Total Carbohydrate, 6 g Dietary Fiber, 10 g Protein, 183 mg Calcium.

VEGETABLE LASAGNA

Makes 6 servings

9 ounces uncooked curly or plain lasagna noodles (9 noodles)
1 tablespoon olive oil
2 medium onions, thinly sliced
1 medium red bell pepper, thinly sliced
1 medium green bell pepper, thinly sliced
2 cups chopped broccoli
2 garlic cloves, minced
1/2 teaspoon salt

2 cups part-skim ricotta cheese
1/3 cup fat-free egg substitute
1/4 cup minced fresh basil
2 tablespoons freshly grated Parmesan cheese
1/2 teaspoon freshly ground black pepper
2 cups tomato sauce (no salt added)
2 1/4 ounces part-skim mozzarella cheese, shredded

1. Preheat oven to 400° F.
2. In large pot of boiling water, cook lasagna noodles 10–12 minutes, until tender. Drain, discarding liquid. Place into large bowl of cold water; set aside.
3. Meanwhile, in large nonstick skillet, heat oil; add onions. Cook over medium heat, stirring frequently, 3–5 minutes, until onions are softened. Add red and green bell peppers; cook, stirring frequently, 5 minutes, until peppers are tender. Add broccoli, garlic and salt; stir to combine. Cook, covered, 10 minutes, until vegetables are very tender. Remove from heat; set aside.
4. In medium bowl, combine ricotta cheese, egg substitute, basil, Parmesan cheese and black pepper.
5. Spread 1/2 cup tomato sauce in 13 × 9" baking pan; drain noodles.
6. To assemble lasagna, top sauce in pan with 3 noodles, overlapping edges if necessary. Spread noodles with one third of the ricotta cheese mixture, one third of the vegetable mixture and 1/2 cup of the remaining tomato sauce; sprinkle evenly with one third of the mozzarella cheese. Repeat layers two more times. Bake 45 minutes, until cheese is melted and sauce is bubbling. Remove from oven; let stand 10 minutes. Divide evenly among 6 plates and serve.

Serving (one-sixth of lasagna) provides: 1/2 Fat, 3 Vegetables, 2 Proteins, 2 Breads, 10 Optional Calories.

Per serving: 390 Calories, 12 g Total Fat, 6 g Saturated Fat, 33 mg Cholesterol, 417 mg Sodium, 49 g Total Carbohydrate, 4 g Dietary Fiber, 22 g Protein, 369 mg Calcium.

SPINACH AND CHEESE CANNELLONI

Makes 4 servings

Cannelloni, sheets of pasta stuffed with a savory filling, are an Italian favorite. By using lasagna noodles for the cannelloni shells we've simplified the process.

4 ounces curly or plain lasagna noodles (4 noodles)

One 10-ounce package thawed frozen chopped spinach, thoroughly drained and squeezed dry

1 cup part-skim ricotta cheese

3 ounces part-skim mozzarella cheese, shredded

$^3/_4$ ounce Parmesan cheese, grated

$^1/_4$ cup minced fresh basil

1 egg, lightly beaten

$^1/_2$ teaspoon freshly ground black pepper

$^1/_4$ teaspoon ground nutmeg

$1^1/_2$ cups marinara sauce

1. Preheat oven to 425° F.
2. In large pot of boiling water, cook lasagna noodles 10–12 minutes, until tender. Drain, discarding liquid; cut each noodle in half crosswise. Place noodles into large bowl of cold water; set aside.
3. In medium bowl, combine spinach, ricotta, mozzarella and Parmesan cheeses, basil, egg, pepper and nutmeg; set aside.
4. Spread $^1/_2$ cup marinara sauce in 9" square baking pan. Drain noodles. Spread each with an equal amount of spinach mixture; roll up to enclose. Place rolls, seam-side down, into pan. Top with remaining 1 cup marinara sauce; bake 30 minutes, until rolls are heated through and sauce is bubbling. Place 2 rolls on each of 4 plates and serve.

Serving (2 rolls) provides: 1 Fat, $2^1/_4$ Vegetables, $2^1/_2$ Proteins, $1^1/_4$ Breads, 10 Optional Calories.

Per serving: 372 Calories, 15 g Total Fat, 7 g Saturated Fat, 89 mg Cholesterol, 935 mg Sodium, 39 g Total Carbohydrate, 2 g Dietary Fiber, 23 g Protein, 510 mg Calcium.

PENNE AND MUSHROOM CASSEROLE

Makes 4 servings

This casserole, made with the ridged tubular pasta called penne *rigate,* is a far cry from the typical baked ziti. Its brilliant fragrance and zesty flavors make it a dish suitable for serving to guests as well as a hungry family.

6 ounces penne *rigate* pasta
2 teaspoons olive oil
1 cup sliced shallots
1 garlic clove, minced
4 cups sliced mushrooms
1^1/$_2$ medium tomatoes, seeded and diced
1 teaspoon minced fresh thyme leaves

^{1}/$_2$ teaspoon freshly ground black pepper
^{1}/$_2$ teaspoon salt
1 cup part-skim ricotta cheese
3 tablespoons freshly grated Parmesan cheese

1. Preheat oven to 425° F. Spray 9" square baking pan with nonstick cooking spray.
2. In large pot of boiling water, cook penne 10–12 minutes, until tender. Drain, discarding liquid; set penne aside.
3. Meanwhile, in large nonstick skillet, heat oil; add shallots. Cook over medium heat, stirring frequently, 3–5 minutes, until shallots are softened. Add garlic; cook, stirring frequently, 2 minutes.
4. Increase heat to medium-high; add mushrooms. Cook, stirring frequently, 3–4 minutes, until mushrooms release their liquid. Continuing to stir, cook 3–4 minutes, until liquid is evaporated and mushrooms are golden brown. Add tomatoes, thyme, pepper and salt; cook, stirring frequently, 3–5 minutes, until tomatoes are softened and mixture is thick. Remove from heat.
5. Add ricotta cheese and cooked penne to mushroom mixture; stir to combine. Transfer to prepared baking pan; sprinkle evenly with Parmesan cheese. Bake 15 minutes, until mixture is golden brown. Remove from oven; let stand 5 minutes. Divide evenly among 4 plates and serve.

Serving (1^1/$_4$ cups) provides: ^{1}/$_2$ Fat, 3^1/$_4$ Vegetables, 1 Protein, 2 Breads, 25 Optional Calories.

Per serving: 342 Calories, 10 g Total Fat, 4 g Saturated Fat, 22 mg Cholesterol, 436 mg Sodium, 48 g Total Carbohydrate, 3 g Dietary Fiber, 17 g Protein, 254 mg Calcium.

BAKED ZITI WITH CAULIFLOWER

Makes 4 servings

A simple white sauce, spiked with robust Parmesan cheese and fragrant nutmeg, makes pasta and cauliflower especially delicious.

6 ounces ziti
2 teaspoons vegetable oil
1 tablespoon all-purpose flour
1 cup skim milk
1$^{1}/_{2}$ ounces Parmesan cheese, grated

$^{1}/_{2}$ teaspoon freshly ground black pepper
$^{1}/_{4}$ teaspoon ground nutmeg
3 cups cooked cauliflower florets

1. Preheat oven to 350° F. Spray 9" square baking pan with nonstick cooking spray.
2. In large pot of boiling water, cook ziti 10–12 minutes, until tender. Drain, discarding liquid; set ziti aside.
3. Meanwhile, in medium nonstick saucepan, heat oil; add flour. Cook over medium-low heat, stirring constantly with wire whisk, 3 minutes, until mixture is golden brown. Remove from heat; set aside to cool.
4. Meanwhile, in small saucepan, bring $^{3}/_{4}$ cup of the milk just to a boil; remove from heat.
5. Add remaining $^{1}/_{4}$ cup milk to cooled flour mixture, stirring with wire whisk until smooth. Continuing to stir, blend flour mixture into hot milk until smooth; cook over low heat, stirring constantly, 4 minutes, until mixture is slightly thickened. Stir in 1 ounce of the cheese, the pepper and nutmeg; remove from heat.
6. In prepared baking pan, combine cauliflower and ziti. Add milk mixture; toss to combine. Sprinkle with remaining cheese. Bake 30 minutes, until top is golden and sauce is bubbling. Remove from oven; let stand 5 minutes. Divide evenly among 4 plates and serve.

Serving (one-fourth of mixture) provides: $^{1}/_{4}$ Milk, $^{1}/_{2}$ Fat, 1$^{1}/_{2}$ Vegetables, $^{1}/_{2}$ Protein, 2 Breads, 10 Optional Calories.

Per serving: 280 Calories, 7 g Total Fat, 3 g Saturated Fat, 10 mg Cholesterol, 239 mg Sodium, 41 g Total Carbohydrate, 3 g Dietary Fiber, 14 g Protein, 256 mg Calcium.

ROTELLE WITH ROASTED VEGETABLES

Makes 4 servings

Prepare this fabulous dish in early autumn, when there is a slight nip in the air but the farmer's market is still bountiful with fresh produce.

6 ounces rotelle (spiral-shaped) pasta

4 large plum tomatoes, cut into thin wedges

2 medium red onions, cut into $1/2$" slices

2 medium red or yellow bell peppers, cut into $1/2$" slices

2 medium zucchini, cut into $1/4$" slices

1 tablespoon + 1 teaspoon olive oil

1 tablespoon minced fresh thyme leaves

3 garlic cloves, quartered

$1/2$ teaspoon freshly ground black pepper

$1/4$ cup finely shredded fresh basil

1 tablespoon freshly grated Parmesan cheese

1. Preheat oven to 400° F. Line large roasting pan with foil.
2. In large pot of boiling water, cook rotelle 10–12 minutes, until tender. Drain, reserving $1/2$ cup liquid; set rotelle and reserved liquid aside.
3. Meanwhile, in large bowl, combine tomatoes, onions, bell peppers, zucchini, oil, thyme, garlic and black pepper, tossing until well coated. Transfer to prepared roasting pan. Roast 15 minutes; toss mixture. Roast 10 minutes longer, until vegetables are lightly browned.
4. In large bowl, combine rotelle and vegetables; toss to combine. Add basil, cheese and reserved pasta liquid; toss again. Divide evenly among 4 plates and serve.

Serving ($1^1/2$ cups) provides: 1 Fat, $3^1/2$ Vegetables, 2 Breads, 10 Optional Calories.

Per serving: 263 Calories, 6 g Total Fat, 1 g Saturated Fat, 1 mg Cholesterol, 40 mg Sodium, 45 g Total Carbohydrate, 4 g Dietary Fiber, 9 g Protein, 90 mg Calcium.

GNOCCHI BAKED WITH TOMATO SAUCE

Makes 4 servings

These wonderful dumplings, made with a tasty combination of spinach and ricotta cheese, are a lighter version of the original.

2 teaspoons olive oil
$^1/_2$ medium onion, chopped
2 garlic cloves, minced
2 cups canned whole Italian tomatoes (no salt added), coarsely chopped (reserve juice)
$^1/_4$ cup minced fresh basil
$^3/_4$ cup part-skim ricotta cheese

One 10-ounce package thawed frozen chopped spinach, thoroughly drained and squeezed dry
$^1/_2$ cup minus 1 tablespoon all-purpose flour
1 egg, beaten
$1^1/_2$ ounces Parmesan cheese, grated
$^1/_4$ teaspoon salt
$^1/_4$ teaspoon freshly ground black pepper

1. Preheat oven to 375° F.
2. To prepare sauce, in large nonstick skillet, heat oil; add onion. Cook over medium heat, stirring frequently, 3–5 minutes, until onion is softened. Add garlic; cook, stirring frequently, 2 minutes. Add tomatoes with juice and basil; bring mixture to a boil. Reduce heat to low; simmer, stirring occasionally, 15 minutes, until mixture is thickened.
3. Spread $^1/_2$ cup sauce in 9" square baking pan; set pan and remaining sauce aside.
4. To prepare gnocchi, in large bowl, combine ricotta cheese, spinach, flour, egg, Parmesan cheese, salt and pepper; form mixture into 28 equal balls.
5. Drop balls, a few at a time, into large pot of boiling water. Cook over medium heat 3 minutes, until gnocchi float to surface; cook 1 minute longer.
6. With slotted spoon, transfer gnocchi to prepared baking pan; top with remaining sauce. Bake 20 minutes, until gnocchi and sauce are heated through. Divide gnocchi and sauce evenly among 4 plates and serve.

Serving (7 gnocchi, $^1/_3$ cup sauce) provides: $^1/_2$ Fat, $2^1/_4$ Vegetables, $1^1/_2$ Proteins, $^1/_2$ Bread, 10 Optional Calories.

Per serving: 251 Calories, 11 g Total Fat, 5 g Saturated Fat, 76 mg Cholesterol, 801 mg Sodium, 23 g Total Carbohydrate, 3 g Dietary Fiber, 16 g Protein, 421 mg Calcium.

Polenta with Mushroom Ragoût

Makes 4 servings

1 tablespoon + 1 teaspoon
  olive oil
2 medium onions, chopped
2 cups low-sodium vegetable
  broth
6 ounces yellow cornmeal
1 1/2 ounces Parmesan cheese,
  grated
4 cups sliced mushrooms

1 garlic clove, minced
1 cup evaporated skimmed milk
Pinch salt
Pinch freshly ground black pepper
2 tablespoons minced fresh flat-leaf
  parsley
1/4 teaspoon minced fresh thyme
  leaves

1. Spray 8" square baking pan with nonstick cooking spray.
2. In medium nonstick saucepan, heat 2 teaspoons of the oil; add onions. Cook over medium heat, stirring frequently, 5 minutes, until onions are softened.
3. Add broth and 1 1/2 cups water to onion mixture; bring liquid to a boil. Reduce heat to low; stirring constantly with wire whisk, slowly add cornmeal in a thin stream to broth mixture. Simmer, stirring frequently with wooden spoon, 40 minutes, until mixture is thickened; stir in cheese. Spoon cornmeal mixture into prepared pan; refrigerate, covered, 1–2 hours, until firm.
4. Preheat oven to 450° F. Spray baking sheet with nonstick cooking spray.
5. Cut polenta into 4 squares. Place onto prepared baking sheet; bake 20 minutes, until edges of polenta squares are golden brown.
6. Meanwhile, in large nonstick skillet, heat remaining 2 teaspoons oil; add mushrooms. Cook over medium heat, stirring frequently, 5 minutes, until mushrooms release their liquid. Continuing to stir, cook 5 minutes, until liquid is evaporated and mushrooms are golden brown. Add garlic; cook, stirring frequently, 2 minutes. Add milk, salt and pepper; cook, stirring frequently, 3 minutes, until mixture is thickened; stir in parsley and thyme.
8. Divide polenta squares among 4 plates; top each with one-fourth of the mushroom mixture, and serve.

Serving (1 polenta square with 1/4 cup mushroom mixture) provides:
1/2 Milk, 1 Fat, 2 1/2 Vegetables, 1/2 Protein, 2 Breads, 10 Optional Calories.

Per serving: 351 Calories, 10 g Total Fat, 3 g Saturated Fat,
11 mg Cholesterol, 347 mg Sodium, 51 g Total Carbohydrate,
4 g Dietary Fiber, 15 g Protein, 350 mg Calcium.

ROASTED POTATO AND VEGETABLE SALAD

Makes 4 servings

This robust salad makes a wonderful vegetarian entrée; smaller portions may be served as a side salad. It's a pleasant alternative to heavy mayonnaise-based potato salads.

1 pound cooked potatoes, cut into $^1/_4$–$^1/_2$" slices	1 tablespoon + 1 teaspoon olive oil
4 medium red bell peppers, roasted* and thinly sliced	2 teaspoons minced fresh rosemary or thyme leaves
1 medium red onion, thinly sliced	2 teaspoons Dijon-style mustard
$^1/_2$ cup minced fresh flat-leaf parsley	1 garlic clove, crushed
3 tablespoons white wine vinegar	$^1/_2$ teaspoon freshly ground black pepper
	$^1/_2$ teaspoon salt

1. To prepare salad, in large bowl, combine potatoes, roasted peppers and onion; set aside.
2. To prepare dressing, in food processor or small bowl, combine parsley, vinegar, oil, rosemary, mustard, garlic, black pepper and salt; purée until smooth or, with wire whisk, blend until thoroughly combined.
3. Pour dressing over salad; toss gently to combine. Refrigerate, covered, 2 hours, until flavors are blended. Divide evenly among 4 plates and serve cold or at room temperature.

Serving ($1^1/_4$ cups) provides: 1 Fat, $2^1/_4$ Vegetables, 1 Bread.

Per serving: 180 Calories, 5 g Total Fat, 1 g Saturated Fat, 0 mg Cholesterol, 347 mg Sodium, 32 g Total Carbohydrate, 4 g Dietary Fiber, 3 g Protein, 39 mg Calcium.

* To roast bell peppers, preheat broiler. Line baking sheet or pie pan with foil; set whole peppers onto prepared baking sheet. Broil peppers 4–6" from heat, turning frequently with tongs, until skin is lightly charred on all sides. Transfer peppers to bowl; let cool. Peel, seed and devein peppers over bowl to catch juices.

LAYERED VEGETABLE TERRINE

Makes 4 servings

1 medium (1–1¹/₄ pounds)
  eggplant
1 teaspoon salt
2 medium zucchini, thinly sliced
  lengthwise
1 tablespoon + 1 teaspoon olive oil
¹/₂ cup minced fresh flat-leaf
  parsley

1¹/₂ ounces Parmesan cheese, grated
4 garlic cloves, minced
1 teaspoon grated lemon zest*
1 teaspoon freshly ground black
  pepper
3 medium red bell peppers, roasted†
  and thinly sliced

1. Preheat broiler.
2. Cut eggplant crosswise into ¹/₄" slices; place in a single layer onto paper towels. Sprinkle eggplant evenly with salt; let stand, pressing eggplant occasionally with spatula, 20 minutes, to drain.
3. Rinse eggplant slices to remove as much salt as possible; gently squeeze eggplant until as dry as possible.
4. Transfer eggplant to large bowl. Add zucchini and oil; toss to coat evenly. Arrange eggplant and zucchini in a single layer on 2 large baking sheets; broil 4" from heat, turning once, 6–8 minutes, until vegetables are lightly browned on both sides. Reset oven temperature to 350° F. Spray 8 × 4" loaf pan with nonstick cooking spray.
5. In small bowl, combine parsley, cheese, garlic, zest and black pepper.
6. Divide parsley mixture into 6 equal portions. In prepared loaf pan, layer half of the browned eggplant; sprinkle evenly with 1 portion of the parsley mixture. Top with half of the browned zucchini; sprinkle evenly with another portion of the parsley mixture. Top with half of the bell peppers; sprinkle evenly with another portion of parsley mixture. Repeat layers. Bake, covered, 40 minutes, until heated through; bake, uncovered, 30 minutes, until mixture is lightly browned. Remove from oven; let stand 10 minutes. Cut terrine into 8 equal slices; place 2 slices on each of 4 plates and serve.

*The zest of the lemon is the peel without any of the pith (white membrane). To remove zest from lemon, use a zester or the fine side of a vegetable grater; wrap lemon in plastic wrap and refrigerate for use at another time.

†To roast bell peppers, preheat broiler. Line baking sheet or pie pan with foil; set whole peppers onto prepared baking sheet. Broil peppers 4–6" from heat, turning frequently with tongs, until skin is lightly charred on all sides. Transfer peppers to bowl; let cool. Peel, seed and devein peppers over bowl to catch juices.

Serving (one-fourth of terrine) provides: 1 Fat, 4$^1/_2$ Vegetables, $^1/_2$ Protein.

Per serving: 173 Calories, 8 g Total Fat, 3 g Saturated Fat, 8 mg Cholesterol, 347 mg Sodium, 20 g Total Carbohydrate, 5 g Dietary Fiber, 8 g Protein, 245 mg Calcium.

ITALIAN VEGETABLE STEW

Makes 4 servings

1 teaspoon vegetable oil
1 medium onion, sliced
1 medium zucchini, quartered and cut into $^1/_2$" pieces
1 medium yellow squash, quartered and cut into $^1/_2$" pieces
3 garlic cloves, minced
1$^1/_2$ cups canned whole Italian tomatoes (no salt added), chopped (reserve juice)

1 cup thawed frozen green lima beans
6 large kalamata olives, pitted and sliced
2 tablespoons minced fresh flat-leaf parsley
2 tablespoons minced fresh basil
$^1/_2$ teaspoon grated lemon zest*
Pinch freshly ground black pepper

1. In large nonstick skillet, heat oil; add onion. Cook over medium heat, stirring frequently, 3–5 minutes, until onion is softened. Add zucchini, squash and garlic; cook, stirring frequently, 4 minutes, until vegetables are lightly browned.
2. Add tomatoes with juice, beans, olives, parsley, basil, zest and pepper to vegetable mixture; bring mixture to a boil. Reduce heat to low; simmer, covered, 15–20 minutes, until vegetables are tender and mixture is thickened. Divide evenly among 4 plates and serve.

Serving (1 cup) provides: $^1/_2$ Fat, 2 Vegetables, $^1/_2$ Bread.

Per serving: 119 Calories, 4 g Total Fat, 0 g Saturated Fat, 0 mg Cholesterol, 302 mg Sodium, 19 g Total Carbohydrate, 4 g Dietary Fiber, 5 g Protein, 72 mg Calcium.

*The zest of the lemon is the peel without any of the pith (white membrane). To remove zest from lemon, use a zester or the fine side of a vegetable grater; wrap lemon in plastic wrap and refrigerate for use at another time.

RED PEPPER, ONION AND POTATO FRITTATA

Makes 4 servings

Frittatas, which are essentially open-face Italian omelets, are wonderfully versatile and make a great entrée for breakfast, lunch or dinner. For an unusual treat, pack them for a very special picnic!

1 tablespoon olive oil
1½ medium red bell peppers,
   slivered
1 medium onion, slivered
½ cup minced fresh basil
3 garlic cloves, minced
4 eggs
3 egg whites

¼ cup skim milk
½ teaspoon salt
¼ teaspoon freshly ground black
   pepper
1 pound cooked new potatoes,
   thinly sliced
¾ ounce Parmesan cheese, grated

1. In large heatproof nonstick skillet, heat 2 teaspoons of the oil; add bell peppers and onion. Cook over low heat, stirring frequently, 25 minutes, until vegetables are tender. Add basil and garlic; cook, stirring constantly, until mixture is thoroughly combined. Remove from heat.
2. Preheat broiler.
3. In medium bowl, with wire whisk, combine eggs, egg whites, milk, salt and pepper; set aside.
4. Add potatoes to vegetable mixture; toss to combine. Add remaining 1 teaspoon oil; toss again.
5. Pour egg mixture evenly over potato mixture; stir quickly and gently until just combined. Cook, covered, 8–10 minutes, until edges of egg mixture are set. Remove from heat; sprinkle evenly with cheese.
6. Broil as close to heat as possible 1 minute, until egg mixture is set. Remove from broiler; cut into 4 equal wedges and serve.

Serving (1 wedge) provides: ¾ Fat, 1 Vegetable, 1½ Proteins, 1 Bread, 5 Optional Calories.

Per serving: 271 Calories, 10 g Total Fat, 3 g Saturated Fat, 217 mg Cholesterol, 493 mg Sodium, 31 g Total Carbohydrate, 3 g Dietary Fiber, 15 g Protein, 188 mg Calcium.

NOODLE KUGEL WITH FRUIT

Makes 6 servings

If you have never tried a kugel, this is the one to try. It has all the components of a satisfying sweet brunch or lunch entrée or filling dessert. It is sweet, crisp, smooth . . . perfect!

$4^1/_2$ ounces wide egg noodles
2 eggs
$^1/_3$ cup low-fat (1%) cottage cheese

3 tablespoons granulated sugar
1 teaspoon vanilla extract
$1^1/_2$ small apples, pared, cored and grated

1. Preheat oven to 400° F. Spray 9" square baking pan with nonstick cooking spray.
2. In large pot of boiling water, cook noodles 5–6 minutes, until tender. Drain, discarding liquid; set noodles aside.
3. Meanwhile, in medium bowl, with wire whisk or fork, beat eggs until just frothy. Add cheese, sugar and vanilla, blending until mixture is combined.
4. Stir apples and noodles into egg mixture; transfer to prepared dish. Bake 30 minutes, until kugel is firm and lightly browned. Divide evenly among 6 plates and serve.

Serving (one-sixth of kugel) provides: $^1/_4$ Fruit, $^1/_2$ Protein, 1 Bread, 25 Optional Calories.

Per serving: 156 Calories, 3 g Total Fat, 1 g Saturated Fat, 92 mg Cholesterol, 76 mg Sodium, 26 g Total Carbohydrate, 1 g Dietary Fiber, 7 g Protein, 23 mg Calcium.

RICE PUDDING

Makes 4 servings

You will be amazed at the flavor of this hearty classic. Serve it to your favorite connoisseur as a dessert or snack; it's sure to win raves!

2 cups cooked long-grain rice

2 cups skim milk

4 pitted dates, chopped

2 tablespoons + 2 teaspoons firmly packed light brown sugar

$^1/_2$ teaspoon vanilla extract

$^1/_4$ teaspoon cinnamon

1 ounce sliced almonds, to garnish

1. In medium saucepan, combine rice, milk, dates and sugar; cook over medium heat, stirring frequently, just until mixture comes to a boil. Reduce heat to low; simmer, stirring constantly, 20 minutes, until mixture is thickened. Remove from heat.
2. Add vanilla and cinnamon to rice mixture; set aside to cool. Divide evenly among 4 custard cups or serving glasses; cover and refrigerate until chilled; serve sprinkled with almonds.

Serving ($^1/_2$ cup) provides: $^1/_2$ Milk, $^1/_2$ Fat, $^1/_2$ Fruit, $^1/_4$ Protein, 1 Bread, 30 Optional Calories.

Per serving: 283 Calories, 4 g Total Fat, 1 g Saturated Fat, 2 mg Cholesterol, 70 mg Sodium, 53 g Total Carbohydrate, 2 g Dietary Fiber, 9 g Protein, 194 mg Calcium.

BREAD PUDDING

Makes 4 servings

Enjoy this luscious classic as a sweet brunch or lunch entrée, or as a special dessert. This version is given a flavor boost with orange spreadable fruit, but feel free to substitute any flavor you prefer.

2 cups low-fat (1%) milk
2 eggs, beaten
$^1/_4$ cup granulated sugar
1 teaspoon vanilla extract
4 ounces day-old or lightly
  toasted Italian bread, cut
  crosswise into 8 equal slices

2 tablespoons orange spreadable
  fruit
$^1/_4$ cup golden raisins

1. Preheat oven to 350° F. Spray 9" square baking pan with nonstick cooking spray.
2. In small bowl, with wire whisk or fork, combine milk, eggs, sugar and vanilla, blending until mixture is smooth; set aside.
3. Spread each bread slice with $^3/_4$ teaspoon spreadable fruit; arrange bread, spread-side up and overlapping slices if necessary, in prepared baking pan. Pour egg mixture evenly over bread; sprinkle evenly with raisins. Bake 45 minutes, until browned and puffed. Remove from oven; let stand 20 minutes. Divide evenly among 4 plates and serve.

Serving (one-fourth of pudding) provides: $^1/_2$ Milk, 1 Fruit, $^1/_2$ Protein, 1 Bread, 45 Optional Calories.

Per serving: 268 Calories, 5 g Total Fat, 2 g Saturated Fat, 111 mg Cholesterol, 259 mg Sodium, 46 g Total Carbohydrate, 2 g Dietary Fiber, 10 g Protein, 189 mg Calcium.

METRIC CONVERSIONS

If you are converting the recipes in this book to
metric measurements, use the following chart as a guide.

Volume		Weight		Length		Oven Temperatures	
¹/₄ teaspoon	1 milliliter	1 ounce	30 grams	1 inch	25 millimeters	250°F	120°C
¹/₂ teaspoon	2 milliliters	¹/₄ pound	120 grams	1 inch	2.5 centimeters	275°F	140°C
1 teaspoon	5 milliliters	¹/₂ pound	240 grams			300°F	150°C
1 tablespoon	15 milliliters	³/₄ pound	360 grams			325°F	160°C
2 tablespoons	30 milliliters	1 pound	480 grams			350°F	180°C
3 tablespoons	45 milliliters					375°F	190°C
¹/₄ cup	50 milliliters					400°F	200°C
¹/₃ cup	75 milliliters					425°F	220°C
¹/₂ cup	125 milliliters					450°F	230°C
²/₃ cup	150 milliliters					475°F	250°C
³/₄ cup	175 milliliters					500°F	260°C
1 cup	250 milliliters					525°F	270°C
1 quart	1 liter						

DRY AND LIQUID MEASUREMENT EQUIVALENTS

Teaspoons	Tablespoons	Cups	Fluid Ounces
3 teaspoons	1 tablespoon		¹/₂ fluid ounce
6 teaspoons	2 tablespoons	¹/₈ cup	1 fluid ounce
8 teaspoons	2 tablespoons plus 2 teaspoons	¹/₆ cup	
12 teaspoons	4 tablespoons	¹/₄ cup	2 fluid ounces
15 teaspoons	5 tablespoons	¹/₃ cup minus 1 teaspoon	
16 teaspoons	5 tablespoons plus 1 teaspoon	¹/₃ cup	
18 teaspoons	6 tablespoons	¹/₃ cup plus two teaspoons	3 fluid ounces
24 teaspoons	8 tablespoons	¹/₂ cup	4 fluid ounces
30 teaspoons	10 tablespoons	¹/₂ cup plus 2 tablespoons	5 fluid ounces
32 teaspoons	10 tablespoons plus 2 teaspoons	²/₃ cup	
36 teaspoons	12 tablespoons	³/₄ cup	6 fluid ounces
42 teaspoons	14 tablespoons	1 cup plus 2 tablespoons	7 fluid ounces
45 teaspoons	15 tablespoons	1 cup minus 1 tablespoon	
48 teaspoons	16 tablespoons	1 cup	8 fluid ounces

Note: Measurement of less than ¹/₈ teaspoon is considered a dash or a pinch.

INDEX